MORE PRAISE FOR *NO HOUSE TO CALL MY HOME*

"Ryan Berg's *No House to Call My Home* takes readers inside the New York State foster care system, where LGBTQ youth who have been abandoned or abused are housed in order to keep them off the streets and out of harm. Residential counselors advise and advocate for these kids, helping them to negotiate institutional red tape, visits with their real families, education, employment, and recovery. Berg's chronicle of the lives of the young residents at the 401 and Keap Street shows how much adversity they face and how much strength they draw from one another. These kids are smart, resourceful, brave, and fierce. But they are also kids. *No House to Call My Home* is a call for greater understanding, support, and advocacy for these children struggling to stand on their own as they 'age out' of the system and enter adulthood. Challenge and change are the daily currency for them. How are they to succeed with so many obstacles? This book offers suggestions and hope."

—D. A. Powell, author of *Useless Landscape,
or A Guide for Boys,* and *Chronic*

"Ryan Berg opens a window into the troubled, often ignored world of New York City's foster care system, and by extension, himself. *No House to Call My Home* is an important work that will be a revelation for many."

—Saïd Sayrafiezadeh, author of *Brief Encounters with
the Enemy* and *When Skateboards Will Be Free*

"In *No House to Call My Home,* Berg has given us an antidote to the numbness that comes with reading the statistics on homeless queer youth in America. He's given us their stories. In harrowing, vivid detail, he shows us, through his own experience of working with them, the lives of these young people of color as they struggle through the neglect of adults, the indifference of bureaucracies, and the harsh realities of fending for themselves in a cold world. Again and again, what they are denied is dignity. Which is what this book tries in its own way to give back to them, and which is what any social cause requires to initiate lasting change—the opening of empathy."

—Adam Haslett, bestselling author of *You Are Not a Stranger Here* and *Union Atlantic*

"Managing to be both journalistic and novelistic, Berg provides intimate portraits of LGBTQ youth who are left to fend for themselves. Compelling from the first page *No House to Call My Home* is unflinchingly candid in its portrayal of a broken system and a broken society where abandoned youth are overlooked. Berg allows the brilliance and resilience of these young people to shine bright. The adversity they face should enrage you; their courage and grace will move you."

—Richard Blanco, author of *The Prince of Los Cocuyos: A Miami Childhood*

"Ryan Berg has transformed his experience of working with queer homeless youth of color into a nonfiction book that reads like a novel—it is tender, intelligent, and addictively engrossing. *No House to Call My Home* is that rarest of stories—it transports and informs its reader, mesmerizing us first with the beauty of its economical prose, and then with its unblinking gaze at these resilient young people. I was so moved, not only by their stories—at turns hilarious, tragic, and hopeful—but also [by] . . . the reality of their struggle, and the broken parts of our culture that create it. With this book, Berg reminds us how radical and compassionate an act storytelling can be. Not since Adrian Nicole LeBlanc's *Random Family* have I been so impressed with a writer's ability to show us unseen lives with grace, respect, and clarity."

—Melissa Febos, author of *Whip Smart*

"In *No House to Call My Home* Ryan Berg takes us into the New York foster care system—where he worked for two years as a residential counselor in a group home for LGBTQ youth of color—and gives us, along the way, an earnest, heartfelt, and deeply compassionate portrait of that most fundamental of human needs: to be loved unconditionally. Berg is a brave and clear-eyed writer, and this profoundly important book should be required reading for anyone wishing to be a better ally—or, for that matter, for anyone wishing to be a better human being."

—Lacy M. Johnson, author of *The Other Side*, a finalist for the National Book Critics Circle Award

No House to Call My Home

NO HOUSE
TO CALL MY HOME

LOVE, FAMILY, AND
OTHER TRANSGRESSIONS

RYAN BERG

NATION
BOOKS
New York

Copyright © 2015 by Ryan Berg.
Published by Nation Books, a member of the Perseus Books Group
116 East 16th Street, 8th Floor
New York, NY 10003

Nation Books is a co-publishing venture of the Nation Institute and the
Perseus Books Group.

Books published by Nation Books are available at special discounts for bulk
purchases in the United States by corporations, institutions, and other organizations. For more information, please contact the Special Markets Department
at the Perseus Books Group, 2300 Chestnut Street, Suite 200, Philadel-
phia, PA 19103, or call (800) 810-4145, ext. 5000, or e-mail special.markets
@perseusbooks.com.

Designed by Jack Lenzo

Library of Congress Cataloging-in-Publication Data
Berg, Ryan, 1974–
  No house to call my home : love, family, and other transgressions / Ryan Berg.
    pages cm
  Includes bibliographical references and index.
  ISBN 978-1-56858-509-3 (hardback) — ISBN 978-1-56858-510-9 (e-book)
1. Berg, Ryan, 1974- 2. Sexual minority youth—Services for—New York
(State)—New York. 3. Sexual minority youth—Counseling of—New York
(State)—New York. 4. Gay teenagers—Services for—New York (State)—
New York. 5. Gay teenagers—Counseling of—New York (State)—New York.
6. Group homes for youth—New York (State)—New York. 7. Residence
counselors—New York (State)—New York. I. Title.
  HV1426.B47 2015
  362.7'86092--dc23
  [B]
                           2015011424

10 9 8 7 6 5 4 3 2 1

For M. S., R. J. P., and G. B.—rest in power
For the youth

CONTENTS

AUTHOR'S NOTE

This book is a work of nonfiction, not journalism. I did not record conversations, conduct interviews, or have access to documents as I was writing it. The people in this book are real. Dialogue was re-created from memory or retrieved from notes I took after the conversations took place. I changed certain details to protect the identities of the youth I worked with. The names of the youth as well as their physical characteristics have been altered to preserve the anonymity of all involved. Names of organizations have also been changed. Writing attributed to others was altered for grammatical clarity. While the storytelling and the lens I look through are mine, my goal is to remain true to the experiences of the youth I worked with while honoring their privacy.

Perhaps home is not a place but simply an irrevocable condition.[1]

—James Baldwin

Home is an idea rather than a place. It's where you feel safe. Where you're among people who are kind to you and if you're in trouble they'll help you. It's community.[2]

—Toni Morrison

PREFACE

There are more than 400,000 youth in the American foster care system today, roughly the same number as the population of Sacramento, California.[3] Foster care, created to protect the welfare of children, is a broken system, hobbled by an outdated bureaucracy, underfunded agencies, and overburdened workers, that frequently produces dire outcomes. Research shows that children placed in foster care are more likely than veterans of war to develop post-traumatic stress disorder.[4] In some states, youth are just as likely to be abused in foster care as they are in the homes from which they were removed. Foster care has also become a gateway to homelessness. Nearly half the youth experiencing homelessness today have had at least one placement in a foster home or group home.[5]

Lesbian, gay, bisexual, transgender, and questioning (LGBTQ) youth, in particular, face significant prejudice and discrimination in foster care. Many queer-identified young people, who are disproportionately represented in the system, report intolerance, physical and emotional mistreatment, or neglect by caregivers or peers. LGBTQ youth are more likely than their heterosexual counterparts to be placed in group homes. An overwhelming majority of those youth in group homes have been victims of violence. The Opening Doors project, which provides tools and resources for the legal and child welfare community, highlights the following statistics: 70 percent of LGBTQ youth in group homes reported violence based on LGBTQ status; 100 percent reported verbal harassment; and 78 percent of youth were removed or ran away from placement because of hostility toward their LGBTQ status.[6] These pervasive negative experiences can have a significant impact on mental health and emotional growth. Until recent years, child welfare agencies neglected to provide accurate policy, best practices training, and guidance for workers or foster parents serving LGBTQ youth. Without cultural competency training around LGBTQ issues, the result has been retraumatization, continued abuse, and prolonged rejection for many young people.

Another pressing and consistent theme in foster care research is the overrepresentation of people of color. Race and class bias within the system leads to youth of color being removed from their homes at much higher rates.[7] Studies have shown that African American youth are more likely than their white counterparts to be suspended or expelled from school or labeled "aggressive."[8] African American youth are also more often given psychiatric medications for contentious behaviors, diagnosed with a mental illness, and sent to juvenile facilities; white youth with the same forceful behavior are more likely to be treated as outpatients and released. The disparities are everywhere, from the way doctors describe identical physical injuries—African American youth experience greater incidents of "abuse," while their white counterparts experience "accidents"—to the way police departments handle marijuana possession (black people are nearly four times more likely than white people to be arrested for marijuana possession, despite similar usage rates). Such actions prompt calls to Child Protective Services. As a result, many youth of color find their entry point into the school-to-prison pipeline through foster care.

The traumas of life in foster care can be compounded for young LGBTQ people of color as they struggle to reconcile their racial and sexual identities. As they "age out" of the system—a term used to describe a youth's departure from a formal system of care because of age limits—they face an indifferent world. Across the country, inequalities in housing, health, educational achievement, and rates of incarceration are staggering. Transgender women—individuals who identify as female but were assigned a male identity at birth—are at a particularly high risk of homelessness. The rate of suicidal ideation among transgender or gender-nonconforming people of color doubled for those encountering familial neglect, as did rates of sex work; rates of homelessness tripled.[9] These problems will persist until we wake up—locally, nationally, and morally—and give a hard, steady look at what is causing them, and then take action to address them.

In early 2004 I began working as a residential counselor and subsequently as a caseworker for an LGBTQ foster care program in New York City. The program was made up of two group homes: what I call the 401, located in Queens, and Keap Street, in Brooklyn. For me, doing this work was a way to re-engage with the world, to give something back. I started as a residential counselor, an entry-level position requiring a high school diploma and a clean record. The job responsibilities included providing on-site direct care to the youth in the group home, prompting them to do chores like cooking and cleaning, helping manage conflicts, and engaging them in healthy activities. As a caseworker I was tasked with goal setting, coordinating services, and monitoring the progress of the youth in the program. The aim is to reunify them with family or provide them with the tools to live independently.

I found myself wholly unprepared for the myriad personal and social issues I would be forced to confront. Thrown headfirst into the work, I found my understanding of racial and economic justice, gender identity, crime, and poverty was challenged at every turn. Facing the realities of these youth on a daily basis deepened my understanding of privilege, social responsibility, and community, and ultimately altered my understanding of myself.

While doing this work I learned the statistics. The data point out a litany of troubling risk behaviors. LGBTQ youth are more likely to use and abuse substances, and they experience sexual abuse, violence, and clinical depression at greater rates than the general population. Research indicates that LGBTQ youth are more than twice as likely to attempt suicide as their straight peers. Risk-taking is typical in adolescence. Couple that with the isolation and rejection many LGBTQ youth face, and self-destruction becomes the modus operandi. Leaning on unhealthy ways to cope with trauma can become habitual, and youth with self-destructive tendencies are more likely to become adults with self-destructive addictions. In trying to show the youth alternatives to sex work, attempting to break their cycles of drug and alcohol abuse, and help build their self-esteem, I was reminded of my own litany of risk behaviors, my own struggle as a young man grappling with identity, and my own tendency to seek solace in drugs, alcohol, and sex in order to mask the pain felt from micro-aggressions and internalized homophobia.

While the LGBTQ movement has made incredible strides in recent years, the neglect of LGBTQ youth issues is astounding. The mainstreaming of queer culture and the fight for marriage equality currently serves as the wheelhouse for the gay rights movement. Mainstreaming, some would argue, leads to greater understanding and empathy. Same-sex marriage affords equal rights under the law. This may all be good and true, but gay rights advocates' interest in blending in with the broader society and their narrow focus on marriage equality have resulted in the neglect of other pressing issues. The narrative of cultural acceptance developed by gay rights advocates and picked up by the media isn't entirely accurate. Yes, LGBTQ folks are less stigmatized, and more visible, but only when safely celibate, coupled off, and mirroring heteronormative values—standards that present heterosexuality as the preferred, or "normal," identity. It's a false sense of acceptance, and social media access allows youth still grappling with who they are to step outside the limits of their communities, to exercise their identity while still being reliant financially on their families. As a result, many youth are coming out earlier, and some find themselves facing family rejection—and subsequently the streets. When 40 percent of homeless youth identify as LGBTQ yet make up only 8 percent of the population, it's clear the greatest struggles the queer community faces are not all oriented around marriage.

Audre Lorde taught us, "There is no such thing as a single-issue struggle because we do not live single-issue lives."[10] LGBTQ youth struggles are intrinsically tied to health care, housing, public safety, prison, immigration, employment, poverty, and homelessness. On any given night there are four thousand homeless young people on the streets of New York City. Nearly half of them identify as LGBTQ, but there are less than two hundred beds available to serve that specific population.[11] The scarce funds and resources available to provide those beds are in jeopardy because of budget cuts and political pandering. On the whole, the mainstream LGBTQ movement does a poor job of addressing the needs of the most visible LGBTQ youth (white, middle-class), and often completely ignores the least visible (youth of color, poor, or transgender).

Sexual and gender identity statistics are not universally collected for national homeless research. Most data come from state and local studies conducted by service providers. Staff estimates are typically used to collect information. Given that many youth do not self-identify as LGBTQ when talking to service providers, staff rely on their own assumptions of youths' identities. This imperfect measurement method leads many researchers to believe that the numbers may actually underestimate the percentage of LGBTQ youth who are experiencing homelessness.[12]

The stories in this book are my effort to allow readers a glimpse into an often-unseen world, to evoke change in the lives of youth left without a home because of systemic failures, abuse, neglect, or intolerance of their sexual orientation or gender identity. I attempted to help them through the hardships they faced, only to find their strength and resilience to be more humbling and edifying than anything I could offer in return. This isn't a story of a white man attempting to "save" or speak for young queer people of color. I do not claim their experiences as my own, but many of them allowed me into their lives, and for that I am grateful.

Facing the realities of these youth daily forced me to recognize how our systems fail our most vulnerable, and how much more needs to be done to provide support. The challenges I witnessed these youth confront would send most adults into a mental collapse. Yet they soldiered on, imbued with a belief that a better life was out there, no matter how bleak their pasts had been.

LADY FINGERS

"Bella inhaled the screen from her crack pipe," Gladyce says.

I laugh into the phone and wait for her to join in, thinking this is a joke, but there is only silence on the other end of the line.

"You're serious?" I ask.

"You better believe I'm serious. That child gone and almost killed herself."

It seems absurd, the stuff of fiction. I didn't even know crack pipes had screens. I want to apologize for laughing, but I know Gladyce doesn't have patience for polite chitchat.

"She's OK?"

"She's at Woodhull Hospital. Took her last night and she don't look too good." Gladyce continues, "Her face was all sweaty, but that could of been the crack. Thought you should know." Gladyce is the senior residential counselor at the group home, and the bravado in her voice leaves no one wondering who's in charge. Sometimes she takes the initiative to call me with updates about the residents. "Update," I've learned, is synonymous with "crisis." Gladyce is fairly selective on what warrants a call: bodily harm, suicide attempts, hospitalization, physical assault on a resident or staff member.

I don't get calls about prostitution or drug use anymore. Those incidents are too frequent, and selectivity on Gladyce's part saves me from information overload. I have fourteen other adolescents on my caseload right now with similar issues, and she knows that I can read all about the typical debauchery in the incident reports. No need to bother me with the petty stuff.

Updates on Bella have become more and more frequent. In a month she will turn twenty-one. I was told that last year for her birthday she wanted a cake with lavender frosting and a Louis Vuitton purse. She got the cake and a gift certificate to the clothing store Jimmy Jazz, which she traded on the street for a few vials of crack. This year there is no question about what she wants. Bella knows what she is going to get on her twenty-first birthday. We've been trying to plan with her for this day for a while.

In the State of New York, at age twenty-one, youth placed in foster care must leave the system. State officials call it "aging out." I worry about all the youth as their twenty-first birthdays approach. The weeks prior to the aging-out date can produce the most stress they have experienced, even if they have a legitimate place to go. Typically, they act out. As their frustration mounts, so does their dangerous behavior. With Bella I am particularly concerned.

When we met less than a year ago Bella wanted little to do with me. She was polite but rarely engaged me past a smattering of small talk and pleasantries. I was the new caseworker, the fifth one in the three years since the program's inception. My social work experience up to this point consisted of eight months as a residential counselor at a sister group home in Queens called the 401. How I ended up doing this work, I really don't know. All I was sure of at the time I applied for the job was that I had recently received my bachelor's degree, I was about to turn thirty, and I was in need of a seismic shift in my life. I had effectively dwindled my days down to waiting tables at a Mexican restaurant and then, as a pastime, drinking scotch after scotch until the blue of morning broke through the night. Often while lying in bed, under the heavy weight of a hangover, I dreamed of being plucked from my life like a chess piece and placed somewhere new.

When I saw the online job listing for the residential counselor position at the 401 one night in March 2004, I saw it as an opportunity to push past the drudgery and seize something new for myself. I had wanted to work with kids, in what capacity I wasn't sure. It wasn't until

I was hired that I realized how underqualified I was. Although I considered myself informed on social issues, I'd never worked with youth before, never paid close attention to social welfare concerns or seriously thought about the foster care system. When asked by friends who still clung tightly to aspirations of making it as artists why I wanted to work in a group home, I answered, "Because I need to serve something greater than myself." It sounded good, and I wanted to believe it was true. Really, I hadn't a clue why I wanted to work with marginalized youth in foster care, and neither did the residents. They dismissed me immediately.

"A white residential counselor?" I heard one resident say to another in the hallway as I entered the group home for the first time in May of that year. "I give him two months." They bumped knuckles and laughed.

The first day I met Bella she was sitting on the living room couch wearing tight jeans and a threadbare halter top. The TV she was watching sat on a lopsided entertainment stand with a missing wheel; the window blinds were bent; the bars on the window were bent; the floor sloped; two chairs against the wall sat unevenly. The "Home Sweet Home" plaque just over the kitchen doorway was intended to soften the institutional feel of the house; instead it seemed more like a reminder of what this place could never become. Bella's broad shoulders curled downward. She crossed her right leg over her left and tucked her foot behind her ankle as she clasped her hands in her lap.

"I hear that you're back in a GED program. That's great," I said as I sat down beside her, hoping she would be impressed that I'd done my homework. She moved away from me to the edge of the couch and rolled her eyes. I was speaking first with Bella because her situation was dire. We had seven months to set her up with the resources she needed. I was to work with her closely in hopes of establishing a discharge plan, which would include getting her set up with employment, monitoring her performance in school, and finding her a place to live after her twenty-first birthday.

Everything I knew about Bella I learned from my supervisor, Jessica, and the case file. She had come into foster care as an adolescent; her only family was a grandmother who lived in Puerto Rico. Bella was intelligent, having taught herself to be fluent in English during her brief time in New York. Of all the residents, she kept to herself the most. As the oldest inhabitant in the house, she claimed to want nothing to do with "these children." I'd soon find out that it was common for her to sit alone on the couch watching a bootleg DVD of *Beauty Shop*, feeding her dream of stardom as the other residents played handball across the street or flirted with neighborhood *chulos* while smoking a blunt on the stoop of the Dominican church. She'd sit with her face swathed in Noxzema, sipping fruit punch and voicing her exasperation to the characters on TV. "You stupid," she'd snap at the screen. "Why you play yourself?"

"Well, I'm excited to work with you, Bella," I continued. "I really want to make it a goal that you get a job. How does that sound?" As the words left my mouth I shuddered at their banality.

Bella chipped away her nail polish for a while, then looked up. "You finished?" she asked. Before I could answer she stood up and walked out the door.

The group home is called Keap Street. It houses gay, lesbian, and transgender youth in foster care and is one of only a handful of such programs in New York City. The kids are anywhere from fourteen to twenty-one years old. All of them are black or Latino. They've been placed in care because they were either neglected or abused by their parents or because their behavior was unmanageable in their homes. Most of them are here because when their sexual orientation or gender identity was discovered, they were again abused by someone at a former group home or thrown out by a foster parent.

There are twelve residents. I read all of their files prior to meeting them. When we met I tried to connect their faces to their stories. Maite is sixteen, with long black hair. She styles herself in a tough way that is contradicted by her eyes. Her heroin-addicted mother died of AIDS when she was nine, and her father was murdered in a gang dispute when she was eight. Junior (his birth name is Sheadon) is a nineteen-year-old immigrant from Jamaica. He was placed in care by the courts because he's been deemed a thief and a liar. He was raised with five siblings in a one-bedroom apartment in the Bronx, and he tells people he's a doctor with houses in Long Island and Florida. Diana, called Crush because she crushes so hard on girls, was placed at the home after a stint in juvenile detention for lifting some sneakers for "a shorty I was crushing on." In detention she got into trouble for flirting with another girl whose boyfriend found out and hit Crush in the head with a brick. Now she has periodic epileptic seizures. Nothing happened to the boy, but Crush was labeled a sexual predator and removed from the facility. Now she's in love with Fasheema, who has a trusting face and a dimpled smile. Fasheema has had to rely on sex to survive in the streets, and she uses her body in the group home to manipulate the other residents, namely Crush.

Pimple-faced and slinky, Christina is a cocoa-colored sixteen-year-old transgender Latina from the Bronx who thinks she's a white girl from the suburbs. Her Britney Spears infatuation is all-consuming. Nineteen-year-old Raheem—thin and attractive, with full, pouty lips—was put into care because he was being sexually abused by his father and then by his foster parents. Both his mother and father have since died. He has threatened to kill other residents, and himself, on more than one occasion. Caridad is squat and stout. She prides herself on not "being ghetto." She rejects the other kids' fashion style—Sean Johns, Timberlands, and Akademiks—and instead goes for anything black and adorned with skulls. Her hair changes color as often as her mood ring. On the day I met her she had a four-inch nail jutting out from beneath her bottom lip. I had read in her file that she's a cutter, and as we talked I saw that her arms were dotted with tiny sliver-scars.

And there's Bella. I'm at the residence the day she returns from Woodhull. When she invites me to see how she's arranged her room, I accept.

"Staff says I should be an interior decorator," she whispers, her Puerto Rican accent rolling her R's like pastries. She smooths out her comforter with large, calloused fingers that end in French tips. She shows me her Hello Kitty ornaments and porcelain cat figurines with real fur. The room is tidy and feminine. She has an eye for detail.

"Touch it, it's like real," she says, pointing to a fake cat. She giggles and covers her mouth with her hand.

Bella wants to pass, but she doesn't. With a quick glance you might not see what a closer inspection reveals. She's constantly plucking, cinching, stuffing, bleaching, and erasing, but she can't hide her Adam's apple, her broad shoulders, her large hands. She fills her bra with socks, tucks and secures her penis between her legs, and tapes maxi pads together and stuffs them down the sides of her pants to create the illusion of hips. On the street she finds someone to supply her with feminizing hormones. Her regimen is uneven; only when she strolls enough can she afford it. The effects are evident: her body softens, her skin blanches. She works hard to align how she feels on the inside with her outward appearance and when a man pays her, I imagine, she feels the warmth of success.

"He likes my hands," she once confessed to me, "he told me so. He said I got lady fingers."

When she disappears from the home, we don't hear from her until we get her call asking to be picked up from central booking. The charge is usually loitering with the intent to prostitute or purchasing narcotics. I'll go get her and she'll walk out of the men's holding area without makeup, clutching her belongings to her chest. She won't speak on the way home.

For months I've been trying to formulate a discharge plan for Bella, scrambling to find anything that could work. She has no family members in New York, no appropriate visiting resources. The waitlists for LGBTQ youth emergency housing programs are through the roof. Plus, Bella's behavior has been so erratic lately, I'm not even sure I could get her to show up. She has no adult figures in her life except for her caretakers in the system and, of course, her tricks.

Her addiction makes it impossible to keep a job. In any case, during a good stretch she can earn double, maybe triple a menial income strolling the streets.

I pat the fake cat. It's eerie, feels dead. I'm anxious because Bella and I need to have a discussion. Time is running out, and she acts as if the impending date is just another day, as if nothing is about to change. If my job is to prepare her and provide her with basic tools of survival, I've failed. She isn't ready for anything. The world will greet her on her birthday with indifference. When everything falls away, she'll have no place to go.

"Bella," I say, "we need to talk." She freezes, doesn't look up. Now that I've started, I have no clue what to say. I'm lost. What option does she have other than calling her grandmother and letting her know the situation?

"I'm not going back to Puerto Rico," Bella quips, flicking her finger in my face. "Abuelita doesn't want me."

"You don't have to go back," I say, "but maybe you should try to get in touch with her."

Bella won't look at me. She smoothes the same spot on her comforter over and over. I know the parts of this story that I've read in psychiatric evaluations and in psychological assessments. I've read lists of events loosely threaded together that lead to a diagnosis. In my head I've reworked those events and rubbed them smooth, like Bella does her bedspread, to find something more, in the hope that not only the victim but also the person will be revealed. I've thought about the numerous case histories in her file, the facts strung together so many times that I've begun to see her life as if I were there.

"I'm not going to Puerto Rico," she says and suddenly pushes me out into the hallway, slamming the door in my face.

The name was Baldomero. He remembers his mother running past him like a crazy woman as he played in the island dirt. She was running, he remembers, her eyes shiny with tears. He remembers her screaming, and Abuelita chasing behind her, a rock over her head.

"How can you do this to your child?" Abuelita bawled and hurled the stone at his mother's back. "You beast!" Baldomero dug his hands into the wet earth as his mother escaped into the thicket of pineapples. "I hope you die," Abuelita screamed. "I pray that New York swallows you."

That is all Baldomero remembers of his mother leaving. He stayed on the island with Abuelita; there was no one else with whom he could live. His father had disappeared a year earlier to San Juan and was jailed on drug charges. Baldomero didn't remember anything about him.

Abuelita's drinking was always bad, but when Baldomero was ten years old it worsened. The smell of rum reminded him of browning butter splattering in a pan as she barked in his face.

"You are such a maricón," she said. "It's because your parents abandoned you and you have no man to look up to. Now it is my job to make you a man."

She corrected his posture and his effeminate speech. She told him to act like a boy, play soccer with the other kids. She cracked a switch across his knees if he crossed his legs and sat like a girl. She hated when he giggled in a high pitch, covering his mouth with his limp wrist. For punishment she locked him in the bathroom, where he stood in front of the splintered mirror, a T-shirt tied over his head that fell like a wig onto his shoulders. He pretended to comb through what he imagined to be long hair as he removed a hidden picture of his mother from behind the toilet.

At twelve, Baldomero went out until early in the morning, eyes traced with heavy black eyeliner, lips smeared red. Tiny bruises, bloomed pansies, dotted his neck and chest. Baldomero started growing his hair; he wore tight clothes he got on the street. He placed rolled socks in his shirts and sculpted them until they resembled small, perfect breasts. This is what pleased the men in town who met with Baldomero secretly in the dark anonymity of night. They praised their little girl, their little Bella, and spoke about love as they pressed him down on the wet dirt. The marks he received from the men and those from Abuelita were indistinguishable.

"I will not have a fucking maricón living in my house," Abuelita said and slapped Baldomero across the face. "I'm sending you to see your real mother. You two deserve each

other." *That winter, Baldomero stepped off the plane in New York. He had left his mother's picture safely hidden behind the toilet, where he could retrieve it when he returned to Puerto Rico in two weeks.*

She looked nothing like what he remembered. Her face was gaunt; her eyes sunk deep in her skull. Her skin was pasty and flaky, not bronzed and clear like back on the island. When he hugged her she stood rigid. Maybe she was sick. The man standing next to her grabbed Baldomero's bag and walked to the terminal exit. He was thick and ugly. Tribal tattoos covered his forearms and bracelets collected at his wrists. Baldomero wanted to know who the man with tattoos was, but he wasn't going to ask.

New York was not what he imagined. There was nothing glamorous or fantastic about this city. The buildings looked old and run-down in the night sky, not unlike the crumbling shacks of el barrio bajo on the island. Exposed metal beams jutted out of junk piles from scrap yards along the side of the expressway, and the horizon glowed in a rusting haze—a mix of street lamp flush and snow. The cab driver wore a cloth wrapped around his head, and a wiry beard dropped from his chin. He spoke to the man with tattoos and his mother in what Baldomero suspected was English. Looking up at his mother he asked what the driver had said.

"He asked where we are going," his mother replied, her words flat, her body listless.

"Where are we going?" Baldomero asked.

"The Bronx."

*It took just four nights for everything to go to hell.
He was in the bathroom trying on his mother's makeup.
Meringue and sour smoke trailed in from the other room.
Baldomero spotted his mother's panties and bra on the tile
floor. He put them on over his clothes and burst through the
door, popping his hips to the staccato tremors of music.*

*"Mira, Mama," Baldomero said. "I'm Bella, the danc-
ing queen." Baldomero heard the tattooed man's voice but
didn't see him coming.*

"Your son is a fucking faggot."

*Baldomero was lifted into the air and slammed back to
the floor. His clothes were ripped from him; he felt a burning
in the arm pinned behind him. Then the burning turned to
numbness as something in his shoulder popped.*

"You fucking faggot."

*His face was flattened against the wood floor; a hand
covered his mouth. He saw small vials strewn under the coffee table. He saw his mother's feet, fixed on the floor, as she
sat frozen on the couch.*

*The police spoke English. Baldomero didn't understand
why they were taking him away. His mother's arms were
cuffed behind her back; she wouldn't look at Baldomero as
they opened the door and took him out into the winter cold.
He tried to stop crying, to quiet himself, but visible breath
continued to spit before him. The lady officer rubbed his
back, whispered, "Calm down, calm down."*

He was being taken to the hospital. The next day he would be referred to the Administration for Children's Services and placed in foster care, where he would remain until the age of twenty-one.

I knock.

"Leave me the fuck alone."

I can hear her fumbling through her things. The sounds of rustling cloth, the hollow clink of porcelain against porcelain. I ask if I can come in, if we can sit down and have a calm discussion.

"Why everybody needs to talk with me? You, Gladyce, Octavia, it's annoying," she says through the door.

"Because we're staff, Bella. We're all concerned. We want to make sure you are as prepared as possible when you age out." The door flies open. She is wearing tight low-cut jeans and a belly shirt that exposes a ring dangling from her navel.

"Fuck you and the future." Her voice has lost its feminine tone and settles into a kind of thunder. She pushes past me and down the stairs. I follow, calling after her until she passes through the front door on her way into the clatter and trill of Brooklyn.

I collapse onto the living room couch. B.E.T. is on the TV, blaring out Fat Joe's shattered beats from blown speakers. Crush and a butch lesbian named Serenity are haggling in the hallway over who is better at fucking Fasheema, while Junior and Maite stagger around the residence in a slow-motion blur—glassy-eyed and dumb from the blunt they just smoked. I'm left in the center of the room. Bella's probably crossing the Williamsburg Bridge now, I think to myself. I pushed too hard.

Two days later, I get a phone call from Gladyce.

"Are you sitting down?" She doesn't wait for an answer. "Bella's back at Keap Street and she's freaking out. She locked herself in her room and had herself some marathon crack binge. Now she's tearing the place up."

When I arrive at the group home the front door is ajar, letting the screams out onto the street. Boys from the handball court are on the stoop trying to eye the action. Bella has Maite trapped against the wall in the living room. Her face is flushed and damp, stubble peppers her chin, and the whites of her eyes shine with a manic light. Staff have separated the other residents, barring them from ringside access. Gladyce sees me and mouths to me that the police are on their way.

"I ain't playing, bitch, give it to me," Bella says.

"You ain't getting nothing, yo." Maite puffs out her chest, stares dead into Bella's face. I notice that Maite's left hand is bleeding, one fingernail ripped off. The other residents are trying to wiggle past staff, chiding, provoking Bella.

"Kick her ass," cries Crush, as the room erupts into hollers. "Flatline her!"

Bella presses her forearm against Maite's chest, locking her in place. I'm shocked by her strength, rock solid, muscles twisting and sinewy. So much energy is spent erasing any sign of masculinity in day-to-day life that this sight, when her focus has turned away from herself, is startling.

"Give me my fucking money," she hisses inches from Maite's face.

Maite is resolute, says no without blinking.

Staff are in all corners of the room, prepared to take Bella down if necessary. She pushes Maite with one final threat, grabs a chair, launches it against a wall, and retreats out the door. Octavia follows her but can't keep up. Bella is gone.

By the time the police arrive, it's over. The room has deflated into murmurs. They ask Maite what happened. She's tight-lipped. One officer takes down names, ages, while the other comments on the new paint job in the living room.

"This mauve trim is so much better than the red you guys had in here before," he says, his hands on his waist. "That was too . . . aggressive. This is much calmer."

The police leave, and it's as if they never arrived. Staff start to pick up the overturned tables, broken picture frames—all the remnants of Hurricane Bella. The residents disperse, leaving the living room empty except for Maite. She is sitting on the couch, clutching her bleeding hand, her chin pressed against her chest. Octavia gives her a cotton ball and some gauze to wrap up her finger. I ask her to go for a walk with me.

"Buy me a loosie?" she says as we make our way beneath the elevated J train along Broadway. She stops outside the corner bodega and puts out her palm. I dig in my pocket and extract two quarters. She plucks them from my hand and runs inside. I don't make it a practice to provide cigarette money for residents, especially those who are underage, but Maite is badly shaken. She exits the store with a single Newport menthol, lights it, inhales deeply, and offers a forced smile. When I ask her what happened with Bella, she becomes sullen and stares at her feet.

"She was fiending, yo," Maite says. "She came into the house all high and shit and asked me to hold her money—two hundred coins—told me not to give it to her no how."

"Where'd she get it?" I ask.

"Some guy she sees on the regular gave her eight hundred dollars and this was all she had left. She was afraid she was gonna blaze it all, that's why she told me to hold it from her. Then she went into her room and smoked the rest of the rock she had. Fifteen minutes later she came into my room asking for twenty, saying all she wanted was twenty, and I was like, Hell no. I said she needed that money for an apartment or something. She needs to think about her future. That's when she started tearing up my shit."

Maite and I stop on the Brooklyn-Queens Expressway overpass and look out onto the cars racing beneath us.

"I hate when she smokes that shit," she says. We make our way back to Keap Street. A train rumbles overhead, a homeless man cradles himself in the doorway of the abandoned movie theater on the corner. The doors are shattered, boarded up. The marquee above, with its missing letter, reads: C OSED.

"I'm proud of you," I tell her. "Bella's going through it right now, and you've been a good friend." I place my hand on her back and embrace her. She smothers herself into me, doesn't let go right away.

As Bella's twenty-first birthday approaches we hold a discharge conference. Our agency support team and the case manager from the Administration for Children's Services—the city organization that oversees foster care—gather in the conference room to discuss planning strategies for Bella. She doesn't attend. She's been AWOL for days. Some of the residents have seen her on the stroll. There are rumors that she's been staying at the Hotel Gansevoort in the Meatpacking District. We begin to talk about her functioning during the previous six months and her discharge plan. Each youth goes through permanency planning meetings twice a year. Most of them refuse to attend even though their participation is considered critical. They know from experience that the gatherings can be ugly, uncomfortable. Adults sit in a room and discuss their cases, offer suggestions, conflict resolutions, speak about the most private moments of their lives, and then assign goals. Each incident is still-framed, dissected, and picked through. I don't blame her for not showing up.

The room is canary yellow. There are pictures on the walls of sunsets, a snowy landscape, subtitled with supposedly inspirational sayings like "Today is the first day of the rest of your life." Workers sit around a conference table and feign interest as I read from the narrative that I've prepared:

> Bella is noncompliant with program rules and regulations. She interacts well with staff and peers but refuses to do her daily chores. Residential staff reports that she AWOLs and breaks curfew with regularity. Bella abuses marijuana and crack cocaine on a consistent basis and self-reports that she prostitutes intermittently although staff believes it is much more frequent. She was arrested three times during this reporting period for prostitution and once for purchasing narcotics. The agency has made

concerted efforts to engage Bella in therapy in order to address her history of family trauma and abandonment but she refuses to comply with recommendations. She also refuses to attend scheduled medical and psychiatric appointments. The Independent Living Specialist made efforts with the caseworker to find gainful employment for Bella and an internship was acquired for her through the Sylvia Rivera Law Project, an advocacy group for transgender rights. She attended the internship for one week and then suddenly stopped. Bella will be turning twenty-one on November 28 and subsequently aging out of foster care. This caseworker has been working diligently to establish a permanency plan for Bella but with little success. She has refused to attend meetings with aftercare programs and assisted living centers, she is unwilling to keep appointments to discuss housing subsides and Section 8 applications. She has no viable visiting resources and is unable to maintain employment past two weeks. The agency has attempted to place her in a detox program to address her chronic drug abuse but Bella refuses.

And on it goes. The details of her life are imparted with dry, curt language. We sum up her existence as a series of failures to comply with recommendations, exposing her tender spots like blisters.

"Are there any positive role models in her life?" asks the ACS worker. She has a Caribbean accent and is over-dressed. A gold chain lies heavy over her blouse. She looks out of place. I'm reminded of the first time I went out with Bella in public. She drew so much attention to herself that it made me uneasy. Sashaying down the street like it was her own personal catwalk. Boys walked by and howled. "You see that?" one said. "That was a dude. Nasty ass shit." She kept walking with her chin high. The boys passed us and one spat at her feet. I pretended not to notice, just looked down and plunged my hands deep in my pockets, fishing for some cigarettes I didn't have.

"The only adults in her life are from this agency and the tricks on the street," I say. The closest we've come to finding housing for Bella is to place her name on the waiting list at a homeless shelter for LGBTQ youth. But the list is long, and the beds are few. There's no guar-antee she'll ever receive housing there. Most transitional living programs won't consider her, and alternative hous-ing resources are limited because of her record. Looking down at my report, I continue, "I hate to plan this way, but I feel like we're out of options." I pause to try and frame the words in my mind and make sure they come out right. "If we can get her to get tested—I know how this sounds—but if we can get her to get tested there are residential programs for people with HIV. She might qualify."

"We can't force her to get tested," Gladyce says. "And she won't do it. We've tried."

"There's little recourse," the executive director of our program says. "The only thing we can do is set her up for long-term drug treatment. She's knocked down all other attempts at permanency planning."

The ACS worker scribbles down her notes. Despite the canary walls, the room seems dark. Her nail polish is immaculate and loud. An imitation jewel is centered at the tip of each nail. She starts to make recommendations for Bella although she's never met her and doesn't understand the first thing about her. She talks about strategy and planning, bank accounts, and job referrals. When she uses male pronouns and refers to Bella as Baldomero, I know she doesn't respect Bella enough to provide guidance. She doesn't understand the difficulties of planning for her. I want to explain that finding her a job will be more difficult than finding one for a typical client. An employer will take one look at her and then at her state ID. *Baldomero?* And inevitably, *I got nothing against you people personally, but we don't want to make our customers uncomfortable.* I want to explain that the allure of the stroll is more than just money. It's the only place where Bella feels accepted. For a brief moment in the arms of a trick she's no longer treated as a freak; she's desired.

I look at the wall, the pale canary. The worker keeps spewing out words that have no relation to Bella: family resources, secured employment. She might as well be discussing stock options or summer homes in the Hamptons. I imagine where Bella is now. I picture her in a room near the piers, maybe with other trans girls. They've scored enough rock to get them roiling. Only a blow job a piece, fifty bucks a pop, thirty minutes out of their day, and they can blaze until their brains ignite, filling their lungs as the world fades away, leaving them to forget all the things they never wanted to be. *Today is the first day of the rest of your life.*

The meeting ends. I make my way down the stairs and push past the door.

I meet weekly with Laura, the program therapist, for clinical supervision. Caseworkers and house managers in our program are offered individual sessions to air frustrations and grievances about the work in a confidential environment.

"How are you today?" Laura asks, as she does at the beginning of every session. She's sprightly and always engages in talk with a puckish curiosity. When we first started having these meetings six months ago I was annoyed with her peppiness, but then I started to wonder if it was in fact envy that I felt. Each week as we begin I watch as the same blond curl over her right eye bobs, just as it did the week before. Her hair is a bundle of controlled chaos.

She asks about my week, and whether I found anything particularly frustrating. I can't think of something specific and grab my water bottle as a distraction, swig from it, struggling to maintain eye contact. I need to answer her, so I make up something about paperwork and the difficulties of meeting deadlines. She nods gently and smiles.

"How do you feel you are acclimating to the position?" she asks. "It's a difficult job. Feeling overwhelmed would make sense." She emphasizes that in this work it is important to take care of yourself. "Have you been going out with friends? Exercising?" I can't remember the last time I did anything social. I seem to have forgotten how. I manage to tell her that I'm unsure how to separate my work from my personal life. I admit that I haven't been tending to myself, as I should.

All of a sudden I feel this swell inside me. I'm unsure how to empower the young people we work with when I am myself weighed down with so much self-doubt. I have done things, too—things that, if ever discovered, might jeopardize my credibility as a positive influence on the youth. But I don't tell her any of this. Sitting back in my chair, I shove the desire for disclosure back down into my gut, keep it buried.

"You are no good to the residents if you don't take care of yourself," Laura says, brushing a drooping curl away from her forehead. It falls back in place.

I confess that I am overwhelmed and that, specifically, it is working with Bella I find most difficult. In the past month I have just started to get close to her. Her guard is finally beginning to drop. She has started speaking about her past, something she rarely did.

"Do you feel responsible for Bella's failures?" Laura asks.

"Of course I do, it's impossible not to." I suddenly feel self-conscious and don't know what to do with my hands. Bella's failures—the part of her that can only accept affection from unavailable men, the part that is restless, empty, that, if left idle, might wither altogether—I know those parts of her. I've met them within myself. I reach for my water bottle and take a gulp. "It's my job to get her to a place where she'll succeed."

"Your job is to provide the tools that enable successful behavior, and you've done that," Laura insists. "The youth come to us fully formed. We can't undo their pasts. We can only hope to help them heal and move forward successfully. But we can't do everything for them; they have to meet us halfway."

Laura looks at me gently until I meet her eye.

"Ryan, whatever happens to her, you've done your part. Now it's Bella's turn. Now she has to come to you."

Two weeks later, Bella is sitting in my office. I can tell she's been up for days. She fusses and struggles to get comfortable in her seat. She seems both wired and sluggish at once. She taps her foot incessantly, props her head with her hand.

"I didn't have to come, you know. I coulda just left out, never come back," she says.

We haven't seen her for days. No phone calls, no visits, nothing. I was starting to think that maybe she met the wrong guy on the pier. Perhaps he realized Bella had a penis and freaked out and dumped her in some alley, or off some pier. Turns out she found a thirty-year-old man from Hoboken who lives with his parents, a guy with a crack habit as chronic as hers and delusions just as grand.

"He loves me," she says. "He gonna give me a car and an apartment. So you do you and I'll do me."

"You've known this guy for how long? A week?" I want to ask if she's high, but I don't.

Her face scrunches. "So?" she says. "You can love somebody that quick."

"Bella, what happens if it doesn't work out?"

"He already showed me the apartment. A guy lives there now but he's moving out soon. It's in Hell's Kitchen. I told him I want new carpet and a wood bedroom set with the thing over the bed, how you call it?"

"A canopy."

"Yeah, a canopy." Her arms reach out as if she's touching it. "And I want nice dishes for dinner too."

I lean forward and place my hand on her knee. She stops fidgeting. "Bella, listen to yourself," I say. "This isn't realistic; it's fantasy. Time is running out. You have two weeks, *two weeks*. Something's got to change or you're going to end up on the street."

Bella becomes motionless as my words fill the space between us. Her legs are pressed together; her arms fold over her chest. She turns her head away from me as she stares out the window. In the muted Brooklyn light filtering through the window, she almost looks like a silent screen star waiting for her closeup.

"Can't you just let me have my dream?"

THE 401

CHAPTER 1

A MEMBER
OF THE FAMILY

The house is mostly silent. Nearly all of the residents are away at school. The only thing I can hear from where I'm sitting in the office is a heavy, low voice. It's coming from the dinner table down the hall. "Not again," I think as I look at the clock: 2:00 p.m. I grab the key ring and get up from the desk.

The venetian blinds are drawn. Thin wedges of sunlight slice through the slats and marble the tabletop. Benny is balancing on the rear legs of his chair. His head is tilted and the telephone is caught between his ear and his shoulder. As he talks he wraps the coiling cord around his finger. A manicured but full beard traces the outline of his jaw and makes him look older than his nineteen years despite his short and stout frame. Benny doesn't look up as I motion for him to hand over the phone.

"Yo, I'm definitely feeling that," he says into the receiver. "For sure."

I can always tell when he's on the chat line because his voice drops two octaves lower than normal. His obsession with talking to strangers on the phone is a growing concern for the staff. He pays for the chat lines with one of the many credit cards he's received, despite not having a job—a detail he's managed to keep secret from everyone until recently. When he maxes out one card, he moves on to the next. This allows him to talk endlessly to anonymous men on the other end of the line, disclosing the most intimate details of his life, letting down the guard he tries to maintain in the group home. The staff has talked with him about the level of disclosure in his conversations, appropriate boundaries, and money management, but he won't have it. He's "all grown," he says. We need to stay out of his business.

"Can I have the phone, please?" I whisper. Benny looks up, doesn't cover the mouthpiece.

"Leave me the fuck alone, son. Can't you see I'm busy?" He winks at me, as if we're both in on a joke, then turns away and presses his lips into the receiver.

"Nah, that just my roommate. He always be fiending for the phone."

Sometimes Benny tells the men that he has his own apartment. Other times he says he still lives at home. But he never mentions foster care or the group home.

When I catch his eye again I smile weakly at him, point to the clock on the wall. He rolls his eyes and looks away.

"Benny."

He ignores me.

"Benny, you can't be on the phone now, I'm sorry."

"Wait," he hisses at me from the corner of his mouth, shooing me away with his hand. "No, not you man," he says into the receiver. "No really, we good. Oh, word? All right, hit me up later, son. No, we cool. Sure, later." Benny slams the phone down into its cradle and glares up at me. "You really know how to get up in my shit."

"I'm sorry, but phone privileges start at 4:00 p.m."

I disconnect the cheap RadioShack model from the wall and twine the cord around. "Ms. Celeste said you're supposed to ask permission before taking this from the office."

"Actually, phone privileges start at 4:00 p.m. *for students*. I'm not a student, so I can use it whenever I want."

In my short time at the 401, I've already learned Benny has a habit of correcting residential counselors and caseworkers on the program's arcane rules and regulations. After living in the system for so long he knows his rights better than most legal advocates. He finds the loopholes and he tends to fabricate others. I've been studying the House Rules and Regulations packet to prepare for a situation just like this. But the circumstances surrounding Benny are trickier. A few months back, before I started working here, his mother died. Complications from AIDS. Now everyone is unsure how to move forward with him, afraid that pushing him too hard may derail all the gains he's made. I haven't been trained to deal with this kind of loss, so I decide to tread lightly and stick to the packet as a foundation for our conversation. My breathing escalates.

"You're right, students get to use the telephone after 4:00 p.m. But cutting class doesn't mean you're no longer enrolled. It means you're truant. You can use the phone after 4:00 p.m. like the other students."

His face reddens. He stands up and shows me his back. I get a "whatever" and a flip of the hand. He moves into the living room, collapses on the couch, and turns on the TV. *House rule: no television during daytime hours.*

Benny tucks a pillow between his knees, flips to the soap opera *Passions*. On the screen a woman is staring into her crystal ball predicting the future to a man with a chiseled, sharp jaw line and a California tan. Her premonition, bleak. In moments like this, I've seen Ms. Celeste—the worker the residents call Mama—simply walk up and unplug the TV and take the remote into the office with her. I opt for a less combative approach.

"Let's put together a résumé for you," I suggest.

Benny's eyes don't move from the screen. The last job he had was at Met Foods down the block. He lasted two weeks until he got fed up with the manager telling him what to do and pushed past him, knocking over a display case of tomato sauce. When the staff asked why he was fired, Benny said, "Some people just don't know how to hear the truth."

"If you're not going to school we should at least prepare you to look for work," I tell him now.

Benny grabs the pillow from between his legs and chucks it across the room. "I can't hear the TV," he says, his face again filling with color.

I'm unsure what to do, so I smile at him. "I'm sorry, but you know the rules. Turn it off, please."

Benny lifts the remote control, points it in my direction, and presses the power button.

"Off," he says.

When Gena, the 401's house manager, hired me in May 2004, she said there was a quick learning curve. No time to leisurely figure things out. "Walk in with confidence," she said. "The residents can sniff out fear. If you don't adapt quickly they'll go for the jugular. Whatever you're self-conscious about," she said, gesturing to my bald head to serve as example, "they'll find it and they'll use it."

It wasn't until Ms. Celeste had me go to Benny's room on one of my first days on the job to wake him up for school that I realized where my insecurity lied. Benny didn't lift his head from his pillow as he muttered, "Go away, tourist." His words shot me outside of myself. I saw this bald, white guy in a dilapidated house in Queens surrounded by kids of color and wondered, "What am I doing here?"

A man from the Midwest with no social service experience, I had no right to step foot inside the 401. And who was I to tell anyone how to succeed in life? I knew from my few weeks of training that a disproportionate number of children in the New York City foster care system are people of color. Although most of the management team in the LGBTQ program, like Gena, were white, all entry-level residential counselors were black or Latino, mostly women. It was obvious a dynamic had shifted when I was hired as a residential counselor. Gena was trying something new: hire someone who seems to care regardless of race, class, or gender. It was an experiment with a high probability of failure. I would have to rely on intuition when feeling out what social workers call "cultural competency." The only guidance I was given in that regard was when I was told not to impose my white, middle-class expectations on the youth. I understood what that meant in theory, but I couldn't envision how that would look in practice. I had to learn on the go.

Gena explained her reasoning for hiring me when she told me I had the job. "These children are in crisis," she said. "Most of them have never been given a chance and have never had any guidance or appropriate attention from adults. Their relationships with family are in ruins, their education almost nonexistent. They've been told their whole lives they're disposable, worthless because of their sexuality or gender identity. Some of the residential counselors here do care, some don't. I'd prefer to have a white guy from Iowa who gives a shit than someone else who doesn't." She paused and looked at me intently. "The youth will push you and push you in order to test you, expecting you to leave like everyone else has. But really they want you to say, 'Keep acting up all you want. I'm not going anywhere. I won't abandon you.'"

I entered the 401 that first day expecting to be introduced to the residents. Instead I walked into a maelstrom of shrieks. All I could make out was that the thick Latino kid screaming and flailing around the room wanted to watch a different TV program from what was on. Instantly I wanted to deaden the noise with a drink. Ms. Celeste seemed unfazed. She walked me through a recital of interhouse feuds, personality quirks, things permissible and things not, as I tried to keep a mental stockpile of everything.

"Don't let the key ring out of your sight. Don't leave the snack closet unlocked or it'll be ransacked. The residents will try to convince you to give them money from petty cash: don't. Don't hand out extra laundry detergent until the first of the month. Sybella can't eat cheese, Montana can't smoke on the stoop, Rodrigo can't be given a home pass no matter how much he persists."

A thin girl in skintight purple jeans and dangly earrings ran up to Ms. Celeste and hugged her tightly, then ran off without so much as a word.

"Touching or any kind of physical contact is discouraged because it can be misinterpreted," she said. "But how are you going to deny a hug from a child?"

Ms. Celeste looked around the room, as if to make sure she hadn't overlooked anything.

"Oh, and Benny," she said, her eyes narrowing, "the one acting the fool about his TV program. Well, Benny's convinced he's all grown now, practically wrote these rules himself, so he thinks he doesn't need to listen to nobody. Don't give in to him."

My shift would be Wednesday morning through Friday night. I'd be the residents' primary caretaker during the day and the sole caretaker during the night. For the entirety of my shift I wouldn't be allowed to leave the premises. The drink I was craving when I stepped through the front door would have to wait.

I knock on Benny's open bedroom door to let him know I'm here. A week has passed since our disagreement about the phone and he still hasn't gone to school. He's standing at his dresser with his back to me, reorganizing his cologne and hair care products. His bed is made and his pillows and stuffed animals are fastidiously arranged.

Barry White's sultry voice comes out of the CD player. Benny loves old-school R&B. Most of the other kids only listen to what's on the radio: Beyoncé, Usher, Alicia Keys. Benny goes out of his way to listen to what he calls the classics: Chaka Khan, Al Green, Aretha. On the wall over his head is a poster of a shirtless brooding man covered in tattoos, arms folded across his thick chest, his eyes narrowed into an exaggerated, menacing glare. His name, The Game, is scrawled across the bottom of the poster.

"Gangster rap doesn't seem like your style," I say, gesturing to the poster.

"It's not but he's hot." I look toward the staircase and back to Benny.

"You know, if you get moving soon you can make it to second period." He continues organizing as if he hasn't heard me. I look to his right, where shoeboxes are stacked as high as his window.

"Can't decide what shoes to wear?"

He lets out a half-laugh.

"Look at all those boxes."

Benny peers over his shoulder. "More than you got?" he asks.

I point down to my battered Converse All-Stars. "You're looking at my whole collection."

He tells me the boxes are filled mostly with Adidas and Nike, some custom designed. Benny estimates forty pairs. Some he's never even worn. "A shoe for every occasion," he says.

"Where did you get them all?"

"Clothing money from the agency, mostly."

I've learned if you want to get Ms. Celeste heated, you should bring up Benny's shoe collection. "We're supposed to be preparing them to live independently," she tells me. "What good are all those boxes of shoes gonna do him? How does having a room full of sneakers that cost a hundred dollars apiece teach him about the reality he's going to face? Show me one unemployed adult with a room stacked with sneakers like his."

Ms. Celeste makes it clear that her biggest frustration with this kind of work is that residents are allowed to remain blind to the veracities of the real world. At the home, they are rarely held accountable for their actions or inaction. It's a life without consequences. She says the foster care system is so afraid of lawsuits and accusations of child endangerment that residential counselors are left with little recourse when addressing maladaptive behavior. The result, as Ms. Celeste sees it, is a slew of young adults launched into the world without the capacity to function in it.

Outside his bedroom door a collage of pictures hangs on corkboard. The images are mostly of Benny throughout his years in foster care, but two stand out. There's a faded photograph with scalloped and bent edges in which a muscular, dark-skinned man with a swarm of curly black hair stands stiffly, holding in his thick arms a small child. They're on the steps of the Family Court building in Manhattan. The faces are hard to make out; the figures, grainy. I wonder if this is the only picture Benny has of him with his father. Is this how he sees their relationship: blurred and distant? The second photograph is a Polaroid framed with glitter and glued onto red construction paper cut into heart shapes. In it, Benny's face is younger, softer. Next to him is a woman wearing an oversized Bart Simpson T-shirt. Her face is sallow and bony; her eyes, drained and impassive.

Benny sees me looking.

"My mom on one of her visits," he says.

She's dying in the photograph, but Benny didn't know that at the time. He tells me he thought she had the flu and couldn't shake it. "When I was born, my dad's girlfriend got jealous and put a curse on me and my moms. I thought her being sick all the time was something to do with that."

I sit down on his bed as he continues to arrange the bottles from tallest to shortest, the warm and bottomless voice of Barry White filling the room. Regardless of his tough exterior, I can tell Benny is grappling with something painful and needs to back away from his life a bit. I want to show him I'm someone he can trust.

I open my mouth, about to try to tell him I'm here for him if he needs to talk, but Benny cuts me off before I can begin.

41

"Don't even bother," he says. "I'm not going to school. You can't make me."

Benny's past comes to me in snippets during weekly staff meetings and on Friday mornings, when Ms. Celeste comes in to relieve me. I learn that he's spent most of his life in foster care, having entered the system at age six. Whereas most residents have a family member the agency plans with, Benny has only his stepfather, a man who has barely showed him any attention. His real father was convicted of manslaughter and is serving a long-term prison sentence. From an early age Benny idolized his father. He'd heard stories about him, how he ran the streets, falling in and out of trouble. The few times the two actually met, the man showed little interest in his son and became annoyed if Benny clung too tightly to him.

Benny is what's known in the New York foster care system as a "freed child." Because there is no family to plan with and because he doesn't want to be adopted, the agency's responsibility is to prepare him to live independently. His stepfather has no legal obligation to Benny because his mother's parental rights were terminated by a court order after she disappeared in the midst of one of her drug binges when Benny was a child.

Jessica, the director of social services, told me that along with the crack cocaine epidemic in New York during the eighties came a glut of new children needing placements. No one had predicted the enormity of the situation, and the foster care system became completely overwhelmed as the number of New York's foster children nearly doubled. Agencies scrambled to find placements, and services were stretched thin. Kids like Benny, caught in the morass of a system in crisis, were, by and large, stranded between going home and finding a permanent placement.

By the time he entered the 401, at age sixteen, Benny had been transferred from multiple agencies, shipped from dozens of foster parents to group homes to a residential treatment center and then back into a group home. He'd been shuffled around so many times that he'd given up on making long-term connections. He was deemed too much to handle for most foster parents. He revolted violently against structure and discipline. Often he became explosive, erratic. He repeatedly tried to run away, back to his mother, even though she barely had running water. He just wanted to be with his family.

Just before he hit his teens his former foster care agency determined that Benny needed a higher level of care and was transferred to a residential treatment center north of the city. The large complex housed what the system calls "hard-to-place" kids. A sprawling campus, it had schools and medical services on site. Although it wasn't a locked-down facility, there were barred windows, regulation plastic bedding, and a confined, institutional feel. Benny later said that when he arrived he wondered if it was similar to the penitentiary where his father lived.

Many of the older boys in the facility used their size to intimidate new residents. They expected this squat Puerto Rican kid with big lips and wiry hair to find his place in the pecking order. But Benny wasn't someone who backed down when threatened.

Around this time Benny started to become aware of his attraction to other boys. He was nearing his teens and the first physical signs of puberty were beginning to show. But the internal changes were even more dramatic. There was no pretending to rein in his anger anymore. It came in sweeping, torrential bursts. One moment he was enveloped in an inexplicable rage; the next he was laughing until his face hurt.

Benny became friends with a Puerto Rican boy named Luis. They slept in the same room, not far from the school. Although Luis was two years younger than Benny, they "grew tight fast." Coming from the same neighborhood, the Lower East Side, they remembered a lot of the same things: playing hot peas and butter and cocolevio. They'd reminisce about how on scorching summer days they drank quarter waters and sat on stoops eating Italian ices. Benny hadn't lived in the Lower East Side since being removed from his mother's apartment six years before, but he still referred to Orchard Street as home if anyone ever asked.

As they hung out more, the feelings Benny developed became increasingly complicated to pilot. At first he didn't think much of the growing need to be near Luis, but over time Benny came to understand from overhearing what the older boys said in the halls that his feelings meant he was a "faggot." He didn't care. His life had always been cursed, so why should it stop now? Although he had never met an openly gay person before, Benny adjusted to his new identity. But there wasn't anyone he could talk to about it. The male staff used homosexuality as a way to belittle the residents, calling the boys faggots if they showed emotion. Some of Benny's peers would become violent if anyone brought up the subject.

Unsure how to proceed with his friendship with Luis, and without a role model to help him answer the confusing questions that faced him, Benny attempted to figure things out for himself. It was obvious that Luis looked up to him. Benny was strong-willed and self-assured and took shit from no one. As the friendship intensified they began breaking off from larger groups to hang out alone. At night he started sneaking over to Luis's bed. They began to fool around and experiment.

It wasn't long before a staff member caught them. At first Benny thought little of it. He'd heard about straight residents getting caught making out, or worse, in the hidden alcoves around campus. As far as he knew, nothing more than a reprimand ever came from it. So when two staff members entered the dorm the next day and told him to pack up his belongings, he was surprised. They escorted him to a room with a single bed, where he stayed until his hearing. Just before his fourteenth birthday Benny found out he was being remanded out of state to one of the few facilities in the country designed to house juvenile sexual offenders. He was sent to a facility down south and labeled a sexual predator.

As Benny sees it this happened because the incident involved two boys, not because of Luis's age. They were both underage. Straight residents were often caught doing the same thing. "Girls even got pregnant. None of them got sent down to fucking bumblefuck," he said.

For a year Benny lived among juvenile rapists with hardly any contact with anyone from New York. He doesn't know what happened to Luis and he doesn't want to find out. It's a time in his life he doesn't care to revisit. He says he's blocked it out. For him, that year didn't exist.

T he week after our talk in his bedroom, I'm in the kitchen making dinner for the residents when Benny walks up to the refrigerator and moves a soda into the freezer. He pauses for a moment and leans up against the counter.

"You gay?" he asks me.

I glance over at him, then back down at the cheese packet I'm opening. "Yep," I say, surprised by the question.

"Well, nobody knew. You don't talk like that."

He pauses again, wipes some crumbs from the counter into the sink with his hand.

"You ever been in love?" he asks, staring down.

"Sure."

"Word. You still together?"

"No, I'm single now."

Benny obviously has something on his mind, but I'm uncomfortable using my personal life as a springboard. I want to be sensitive to appropriate boundaries, and am still feeling out which level of personal disclosure I'm comfortable with. I want to be available, to help, without prying too deeply or exposing too much. When I ask if he's dating anyone, Benny's face lights up.

"I been talking to this guy now for about a week." He tells me he was instantly smitten with his gravelly voice.

"He's heavyset too," Benny says, "just like I like my men."

According to Benny most conversations on the chat line are about sex, but this man, Marshall, was different. He asked questions and patiently listened as Benny talked. He responded to Benny with thoughtful remarks. The more they talked, the more convinced Benny became that he'd found the man of his dreams. They decided they had to meet and planned a date for tonight at the Jamaica Center Mall. Marshall lives in nearby Flushing and works as a janitor at a public high school. He's in his early forties, the same age as Benny's father, and has never been married, although he occasionally dates women.

"He's on the down-low," Benny tells me. "He ain't gay." The down-low, or the DL, is a term I learned from working at the 401, though the concept isn't new to me. Many of the gay male residents are drawn to men who live duplicitous lives.

I move the pot of boiling macaroni over to the sink and dump it into the plastic strainer. Steam funnels up and fogs my glasses. I remove them, turn toward him, and wipe the lenses with the bottom of my shirt.

"Just because he's too ashamed to tell people doesn't mean he's not gay," I say. It sounds glib coming out of my mouth. "Grab me the butter, please."

Benny opens the refrigerator and fingers through the inside of the door, tosses a half stick my way. "He's not ashamed of nothing, it's just nobody's business."

This kind of thinking infuriates the administrative staff of the program. Laura, the program therapist, has told me that down-low culture is a denunciation of everything the gay rights movement has worked for: the call for equality, the right to live openly without fear of being shamed or ridiculed.

"So you're saying you're only gay if people know you have a same-sex relationship?" I feel like a hypocrite playing devil's advocate, but I'm not willing to let this go without challenging Benny's newfound perception of his identity. I mix the butter in with the noodles. I ask Benny to get me the milk.

"Marshall's into dudes but he ain't *gay*," Benny says and lets his wrist flop to accentuate his point. "He don't live the lifestyle."

"Don't let him get you thinking that being openly gay is a bad thing."

He slaps the milk on the counter, barely holding back his frustration with me.

"Maybe it is," Benny says. "Marshall said maybe I'm not all gay," he makes jazz hands, "like I thought."

I stop what I'm doing.

"I'm not into all them fairy-ass niggas," he continues. "You don't see me waving no rainbow flags."

I want to remind Benny of the picture tacked up on the corkboard in the office of him at last year's Pride Parade, literally waving a rainbow flag, but don't. I understand this aversion; I've felt it myself. Although he rarely passes on the street as straight because of his swishy gait, he seems bolstered by the idea that he does. I know the satisfaction he feels blending in. He's equating passing as straight with power. I don't want to push Benny away from feeling like he can discuss relationships with me, so for now I drop it.

"Be careful tonight," I say. He gives me an annoyed squint.

"Call me when you get to the mall." His curfew is set at eleven o'clock but he'll most likely stay out later, and I want to know where he's going. Although I don't agree with this setup, Benny has reached the age of consent. There's little I can do.

"Be safe, have a good time, and bring condoms in case things become sexual."

Benny rolls his eyes and throws his hands in the air. "Why you got to be like that?" he asks.

Although Benny prefers meeting men on chat lines, hearing what their voices might reveal, most of the gay male residents choose the anonymity of websites when cruising for sex or trying to bond. There are numerous sites designed to look like hypersexualized versions of familiar social networking sites. Johnell, a resident close to aging out, frequently sneaks on to Adam4Adam when using the office computer. In New York this site caters to mostly black and Latino men and their admirers. The profile pictures are typically explicit, as are the descriptions of personal proclivities: "Hung black dudes only," "Puerto Ricans and Domincans a +++." At times, internalized homophobia is exposed through personal desires: "DL brothas only," "Masculine only, no faggots." I've caught Johnell more than once staring at the screen, his striking hazel eyes perusing profiles for long stretches, and engaging in flirtatious chats when he's supposed to be searching for apartments and submitting his résumé for jobs. Many men claim to be HIV negative online, either lying or not knowing their true status, while actively seeking out partners for "anything goes" sex.

I'm torn about the youth connecting online. Although the isolation many young people feel while struggling to create an identity can be lessened through conversations with others who share similar feelings, the medium also opens them up to predators who are willing to exploit their youth and naïveté. With all the time Johnell has spent in foster care and social service programs, he's educated about HIV and safe sex practices. Still, he's confessed to me that having that knowledge didn't stop him from engaging in unprotected sex. The promise of attention, of being desired, confused his ability to reason, and emotion took over. He recently tested positive for HIV. Johnell met the man online. The Internet can be a fast track to sexual activity when the young person hasn't fully processed the difference between cyber fantasies and the consequences that can come from engaging in the real thing.

Johnell will be leaving the program soon. I'm concerned about how he'll navigate life without the resources here, and how he'll adhere to the medication regime that keeps him healthy. I try to press back my fears for him, and for Benny. They're both so eager to please, to find someone—anyone—to accept them. I'm afraid their naïveté will be used against them.

I'm out on the stoop, smoking. The dull thudding of the residents' roughhousing is coming from the living room. Above me, past the outstretched tree branches, a few stars emerge like cinder pinpricks through the blue-black sky. I'm sitting with my back against the screen door, taking deep drags from my cigarette. I run my fingers down to the key ring clasped to the belt loop of my shorts to make sure it's there. I can't believe I lost it, even after Ms. Celeste's warning that it could lead to disastrous consequences.

I must have set it down on the counter without thinking when I prepared dinner. By the time I'd served the macaroni and cheese and broccoli, I'd forgotten about the key ring and didn't realize someone had swiped it until I went to unlock the office. It was too late. I ran downstairs and found the snack closet door wide open, the shelves torn through as if by a feral badger. Boxes of cookies splayed open, mostly emptied. Bags of chips, ransacked. Cases of soda, vanished. A month's worth of food, gone. Next to the ripped-open Little Debbie Oatmeal Creme Pie cellophane wrappers was the missing key ring.

Of course no one did it. I questioned all the residents and received nothing but repressed grins and reassurances of knowing nothing. As far as incidents go it's fairly benign, but it's my first one and I can't help but feel deceived. I believed I had gained the trust of the residents in the few short weeks I'd been working at the 401.

I felt ashamed of my ignorance. When no one came clean about who was to blame I tried to assert some authority and told them all to go upstairs. Bedtime would be an hour earlier than normal. Everyone snickered and ignored me.

I blow out a funnel of cigarette smoke, watch it churn in the pale porch light. I gave a one-year commitment to Gena, but I'm not sure I'm cut out for the job. I'm afraid I'll have to quit. My being here would make sense if there were some direct link from my life to this work, if my own family were abusive, homophobic. If, as a child, my father had stormed into my room in a drunken rage or my mother had been a cold and vindictive woman, my choice to seek this out would be understandable. But my parents are loving. I've never known what it's like to experience the systemic oppression, or the pain of abuse and neglect that Benny and the other residents have had to endure.

A car turns the corner, its headlights flash across my face. When it pulls into the driveway I stamp out the cigarette and drop the butt into the ashtray mounted next to the door. Benny gets out of the passenger's side and walks toward the house. He's back from his date on time. I try to get a glimpse of Marshall but can't make him out through the glaring headlights. Benny turns and waves as the car pulls out of the driveway. A thick arm extends from the driver's-side door, waving back.

"What you doing out here?" Benny asks me, making his way up the steps.

"Getting some air."

When he asks why I'm alone, I mention there was a slight incident. We can hear the other residents hollering at the PlayStation inside.

"Early bedtime was their punishment, but no one listened."

I quickly change the subject and ask about his date. He says Marshall was better than expected. A real gentleman. Most men go through with a date only to ensure something will happen at their place afterward, but Marshall got him home by curfew. Benny is curious about what he's missed tonight at the house and needles me to disclose the drama. I tell him about the missing key ring, the ransacked snack closet.

He laughs. "That's it?" I must not be able to hide the hurt on my face and Benny sits down next to me on the stoop.

"You know it ain't personal." He tells me this is one of the ways to break in new staff, see what they can take. "You need to toughen up if you going to last. Stop being so soft or you really going to get punked."

In the office the next day, Ms. Celeste is looking through the logbook. She asks me about the stolen keys and snack closet incident and wants to know how I rectified the situation. I tell her I tried.

"They wouldn't listen to me," I say, and mark down medications on the distribution sheet.

Ms. Celeste looks up from the logbook. "They wouldn't, would they?" She clears her throat. "Stand up."

I glance up from my work. "What?"

"You heard me, stand up."

I rise obediently from my seat. I let out a quick laugh, cross my arms. My weight shifts.

"Now I'm going to go ahead and guess six foot, maybe an inch or two more."

I nod.

"How much you carrying? Around two hundred?"

"About that."

Ms. Celeste snorts. "So you're telling me these children won't pay no mind to your six-foot, two-hundred-pound self but they got no problem listening to my scrawny bag of bones?"

I'm offended and want to say her definition of scrawny must differ from mine. Instead I half-shake my head and let out a weak, "What?"

"How you going to keep asking me *what* like you don't understand English?"

My eyes drop to the carpet.

Ms. Celeste leans in. "Listen, there are plenty of lazy workers who come through here just to watch their TV programs and gather a paycheck that the kids can pull one over on," she says, tapping the tip of her pen against the log. "And I know an educated white boy like yourself isn't here for the eleven dollars an hour they're giving you. I can tell you're here for a reason. Look at me."

I raise my chin, meet her eye.

"These children have enough obstacles in their lives. They're black, brown, poor, and gay. Now tell me that ain't a bad hand. Being easy on them to stay popular in the house only shows we don't care enough to set them straight on what's what. If nobody calls them out on their shit in here, how they supposed to be ready when someone does it out there?" she asks, pointing toward the window with her thumb. "They never been showed respect. So how they going to learn to be respectable?" Ms. Celeste sucks her teeth. "Us, that's how. You're nice, that's good. You have a good heart, that's good too. But these children don't need you to be their friend. They need you to be an adult. Be supportive, give them structure, there'll be push back. But if you stick around, eventually they'll show you loyalty like you never seen. You need to stop worrying yourself if they like you or not. This ain't about you. Don't go treating these children like they're your friends and don't go smothering them with all kinds of artificial affection. You smother pork chops, not children."

Without glancing over to me she says, "That's all I got to say." She slides the petty cash box close to her and begins to count out bills. "Go ahead now and sit your butt back in that chair. You got work to do."

Benny's room is a disaster. Still in his pajamas, he sits on the edge of his unmade bed. His shoulders are slouched, his head angled down. It's two in the afternoon on my day off. I agreed to take him to the YMCA today. Benny said he wanted to get in better shape for Marshall. Although I don't approve of their relationship, getting Benny out of the house and active is important, so I agreed. When I arrived at the 401 I called up to him, but there was no response. I went upstairs to see what was the holdup. His door was open.

Shoes and boxes are everywhere. Clothes lie all over the floor in knotted piles. Normally Benny has the stereo blasting his classic tunes, but today it's quiet.

"I'm not going," he says without looking up. Benny turns his head in my direction, spits on the floor, and looks away.

"Why are you acting like this?"

He doesn't answer.

"You know, you're getting too old for this," I say, trying out my new adult voice. "Don't expect me to do this again."

I turn to leave his room when I notice a letter on his nightstand next to a stack of CD cases and some balled-up Kleenex. Benny sees me looking.

"Read it if you want." He shifts his body so he's facing away from me. There's a silence between us. "I want you to read it," he says.

If I hadn't noticed the heading, "Dear Son," I would have thought a child had written it. First, Benny's father pays his condolences to his son for the loss of his mother. An old friend from the block had written to him in prison and informed him about her passing. He heard she'd had a hard time of it and said, whatever their differences, she didn't deserve to feel that kind of pain. He apologizes for not writing much over the past ten years. There were some things he needed to figure out. The guy from the block had written about other stuff too, said he had some other news. He told Benny's father that people had been saying his son had turned all faggot and didn't even try to hide it.

I look up. Benny is watching me with a flinty expression on his face. I continue reading. His father had found God in prison, and the Bible is clear about homosexuality. Benny's life is immoral. Until he changes his ways he no longer has a father. As long as Benny lives this way he's dead to him. The letter ends, "Good luck!" And, "Remember I love you!" I shuffle the small pages in my hands for a moment. I look out his bedroom door hoping Ms. Celeste will come upstairs and save us both from this conversation, but I know that's not going to happen and I turn back to Benny.

"I don't mean any disrespect towards your father," I say, and fold the letter up, place it in the envelope, "but all of this is coming from a man who's murdered someone. He has little room to pass judgment on other people."

When Benny doesn't respond I get nervous and keep talking. "Some people use religion to justify their intolerance. It's easier for him to face what he's done if others can be condemned too."

Benny's face remains stiff and I realize my mistake. I stop searching for the right thing to say. He isn't looking for answers. I lean over to him and place my hand against his shoulder. His body is rigid, he jerks away.

"Whatever," Benny says, staring down. Then his shoulders begin to shake. He covers his eyes with his hand. I lean down, about to place my hand on his back again, when I see the corners of his mouth turned up, then a quick glance from his eyes. He's not crying; he's laughing.

"Damn," he says, lifting his head, "this is too fucking easy with you." He's pointing at me with one hand, holding his belly with his other. "You such a punk."

Benny falls back on his bed. He continues laughing hard until no sound comes out of his mouth. But his manufactured amusement can't cover up the despair he's trying to hide. Tears begin to streak the sides of his face. He wipes his cheeks and catches his breath.

"Shit," he says, "it's not like I knew him anyhow."

The screen door lets out a slow hiss as a man walks into the house with an exaggerated gait and shakes my hand. Bautista has on his fitted Yankees cap shifted to the side. Stubble speckled with flecks of gray covers his chin.

"My peoples, my peoples," he says as the screen door slaps shut behind him.

Montana and Rodrigo, thumbing their PlayStation controllers, lift their chins an inch to acknowledge him, never taking their eyes off the screen.

Bautista glances around the room. "Time to get this party started." Every Thursday night he comes to the house to host his weekly drug prevention group with the youth. He's studying to be a substance abuse counselor, and is a recovering heroin addict in his late forties. After some urging the video game is put on pause and the residents gather on the couch and floor. I make my way into the office to catch up on my logbook entries. Their conversation drifts in through the open door. The residents focus on the irritations of living at the 401. The grumbling is typical of any teenager who wants more agency over his life. Rodrigo's frustrated that he can't spend weekends at his mother's house because of a court order and pending criminal case. Reginald wants to stay out later with his boyfriend but knows he'll get a "level drop"—an arbitrary gauge of the youths' behavior, ranking them as either "Success," "Concern," or "Alarm"—if he comes in past curfew. Montana starts to rip on how she has to do chores. "Staff is getting paid, why don't they do the fucking chores? It's not fair. This place ain't fair."

I hear Bautista say something to Benny. There's a murmur.

"Come on now, get whatever's bothering you out in the open," Bautista says. "This is time to talk."

When I first met Bautista I was jealous of how the youth flocked to him. He's relatable in a way that I never can be. His story is familiar to a lot of them. He knows the poverty, the racism, the abuse they've experienced. He's done time. Many of their parents are incarcerated on drug charges, and come from similar backgrounds. So when he opens up to them in his informal group and tells them about his recovery, about making amends to his children for fucking up their lives, it resonates. As he talks you can almost hear in their silence a secret hope that one day they'll have a similar experience with their parents.

Benny is particularly drawn to him. He calls him Pops. Many of the problems Benny brings to him are about relationships with men. Bautista never condescends or devalues Benny's experiences because he's gay. When the conversation turns to sex, he offers steady, sound advice.

When Bautista's drug prevention group is over Benny knocks at the office door.

"It's OK if I go out and sit in Pop's car?" he asks me. "There some private things I need to talk about." His features are soft.

"Sure. Anything I can help you with?"

Benny doesn't look at me, shakes his head slowly. "Nah."

"OK." I feel my smile pressing too wide. "Just be back inside by curfew."

Benny nods and walks back into the living room.

When Gena calls for the nightly update, she asks to talk to Benny about a petty cash request he made. I take the cordless phone and walk into the living room. Montana and Rodrigo are back to shooting people up in front of the TV, their thumbs jabbing at their controllers. Reginald is watching from the couch. He rests his chin in the crook of his elbow on the armrest.

I push open the screen door. Moths flutter around the watery burn of the porch light. The twitter of crickets comes from the dark yard. Under a funnel of streetlight I see Benny and Bautista sitting in a beat-up Ford Escort. Benny's face is buried in his hands, his shoulders are heaving. The man he calls Pops rubs Benny's shoulder, his head shaking slowly.

A week later, Benny is draped over the living room couch, craning his neck toward the window air conditioner, which is spitting out a piddling breeze. It's ninety-some degrees. The humidity is an affront, a wall. The brown button-down shirt he received as a gift from Marshall is mottled with sweat marks. He's just come back from his interview with an office supply store. With three bus transfers, his commuting time was almost two hours.

In this heat the overcrowded buses are oppressive. I was surprised when he stepped out of the house this morning. I thought for sure when he met the scorching air at the doorstep he'd just say, "Screw it" and turn back.

Something happened after he received the letter from his father and had his talk with Bautista. He decided he wanted a better life than his family had. I sat down with him at the computer one night and helped write out his résumé. Because his work experience was so infrequent we focused on the time he'd spent as a peer educator, talking to other youth in foster care about HIV prevention.

A lot of preparation went into Benny's interview. We practiced coming across as confident but not cocky. He participated in a mock interview and answered questions. By the time he'd pressed the dress shirt and creased his pants, manicured his nails, and had run out to the barber for a shape-up, he felt prepared. I sent him off with a Metro card and lunch money expecting he'd return with some encouraging news.

"I didn't want to work for that ghetto-ass place anyhow," Benny says, blinking the sweat out of his eyes. "Them faggots don't know shit."

"Come on, now."

When Benny arrived at the store he remembered to make eye contact, shake the man's hand firmly, and smile. The manager looked over Benny's résumé and said all applicants had to fill out an online questionnaire.

When the survey appeared on the computer monitor in front of him, a dazzling graphic announced that he was one step closer to becoming a "member of our family." He whizzed through multiple-choice questions about how to greet customers, how to address discrepancies, how to work within the chain of command.

During our tutoring in the office I said a lot of the questions he'd be asked were common sense. I'd read somewhere that people mess up in job interviews most often due to overthinking. Be yourself, I assured him, and you'll do fine. So when the manager informed him he'd answered one of the red-flag questions incorrectly and they'd be unable to conduct an interview, Benny was confused. The question asks the applicant to put himself in a hypothetical situation. Say you have a friend who is also a co-worker. Say this friend tells you he's been having financial problems lately and reveals that he's been stealing from the store in order to make ends meet. Do you: *A) Report your friend to your boss,* or *B) Keep your friend's secret?*

Benny takes the paper towel I've brought him from the kitchen and dabs the shine from his neck.

"Tell me you didn't," I say, and sit down on the arm of the sofa next to him.

"What? You wouldn't help your boy? The company ain't going to miss nothing. Hell, they don't even know shit's gone missing." I tell him businesses aren't concerned about fostering friendships. They want the loyalty of their employees to reside with them, not some co-worker with sticky fingers.

"But how can they trust someone who snitches on his own peoples?" He shakes his head. "I ain't no snitch and if that's what they looking for then they can keep they dumb-ass job. *Member of our family*, my ass. Them niggas don't have no fucking clue about family."

I t's the morning of high school commencement and Benny's talking on the resident phone in his gravelly voice, absentmindedly staring down at his fingers. Around him, the house is a spate of commotion. Montana is running from room to room searching for her cap and gown. Sybella is arguing on the office phone with her mother, who was supposed to be here an hour ago. And Reginald is in the bathroom screaming because his hair won't set into the perfect wave. Music is blasting from multiple bedrooms upstairs, all playing different songs, while Benny sits motionless, the phone receiver snug against his ear. He has decided he doesn't want to go to Montana's commencement. He says he isn't feeling well.

"Now you're sure?" Ms. Celeste asks Benny, coming out of the office, adjusting her earring. "I know Montana would appreciate it if you came."

"Nah," he says, and hangs up the phone, then mutters something about a sour stomach.

The office phone rings. Ms. Celeste begins to walk in its direction, then pauses.

"You good?" she says, looking to Benny.

"Yeah, Mama, I'm good," he says and wraps his arms around his thick middle. Ms. Celeste holds him in her sights for another moment, then walks to the office to answer the phone. I take advantage of the momentary silence and ask how's he's doing. Benny shrugs his shoulders then lets his head drop; he buries his hands into his pockets and sniffs.

"I dunno. I'm OK, I guess." He glances in my direction. "I just really need support right now," he says. "But everybody's taking off today."

His bottom lip begins to quiver and his eyes are downcast. I let the pause grow between us as I search his face. Finally I say, "You need to build up your repertoire. You're shtick is getting a little predictable."

Benny looks up, a wide smile brandishes across his face.

"Damn, Ryan. You got mad jokes. That shit is funny," he says. "You finally catching on."

Benny extends his fist, we bump knuckles, and for the first time since arriving at the 401, I feel like I might be able to do this work. But I also know there's truth behind what Benny said. His job prospects have dwindled and I know his relationship with Marshall has fizzled because he's back on the chat line, talking endlessly to strangers. He opened up only once with me about the prickly nature of their relationship before it ended. He said Marshall had initially been warm and passionate, saying he wanted a relationship, but then something happened. Benny wouldn't go into much detail but he mentioned something about how Marshall's sister made an unexpected visit while he was there. What happened afterward was murky. Benny alluded to Marshall flying into a rage, berating Benny for being careless. Soon after that incident Marshall began pushing Benny away, always hinting for him to leave after sex, saying he had work to do.

"Yo, no lie, I'm tired of bitch-ass niggas," Benny said. "He played me and split."

Although he's used to this experience when it comes to dating, it always hurts. Benny is attracted to older men and continues to look for one that wants him for more than just sex. Each night he searches the chat line for the man to save him from his loneliness, his ear pressed tight against the phone.

"It's for you," Ms. Celeste says, her hand cupped over the mouthpiece. She wiggles the receiver. "Benny."

He pulls himself up off his chair and shuffles over, grabbing the phone from her. Benny presses the receiver to his cheek. "Yeah?" he says, and disappears into the doorway.

Before I can ask who called, there's a scream coming from the office. Benny bursts through the doorway with the receiver clutched in his palm, his eyes are bulging and wild, like someone being choked. I think something is wrong until he inhales deeply and I realize he's laughing.

He holds his belly and tips his head back, and lets out a howl. "I graduated!" That was his teacher. They have a cap and gown waiting for him. She told him he can walk with his class. He grabs his hair with his hands. "I'm buggin, yo!"

Benny comes up and smothers himself into Ms. Celeste. He then wraps his arms around my ribs, tries to pick me up. I'm stunned, speechless.

"Now you wish you cleaned up when I told you to," Ms. Celeste says. "Better tell Montana to hurry up so you got some hot water to wash your butt." Benny launches up the stairs. I can hear him bellowing about his phone call to the other residents. I turn to Ms. Celeste, who seems to anticipate my question.

"They just got sick of having him. Happens some-times. They didn't want a twenty-year-old senior, I guess. Poor kid, even when something goes his way, it's got to be all lopsided and broken."

I grab the resident's phone from the table, coil the cord around and carry it back into the office. I place the phone on top of the photocopy machine, where Benny will grab it tonight when he gets home. He'll call the chat line and celebrate by finding some older man living on the down-low who'll invite him over.

After I've moved on from the 401, the staff will continue to push Benny to lessen his use of the chat line. But it'll still be another eight months before he abruptly stops after hearing about the Brazell murder. In February 2005, Rashawn Brazell, another nineteen-year-old in New York, was dismembered, his body parts stuffed in garbage bags, strewn all over the city's subway stations. Investigators suspected the killer met him on the same chat line Benny uses. The case was briefly mentioned in the media, and then quietly disappeared. The murderer was never found, nor, sadly, was Brazell's head. Benny will stop calling for a while after hearing about the murder but then, according to staff reports, he'll pick up the phone again.

More than a year will go by before Benny starts preparing to age out of the group home. Because he won't have a job or any money saved, he'll have to move in with his stepfather in his one-room studio in the Lower East Side. The room will be cramped and infested with cockroaches. He'll sleep with a hat on so they don't crawl in his ears. One of his stepfather's friends will sleep there too, leaving Benny sequestered to a small corner of the room, behind a makeshift wall constructed from all his shoeboxes.

He will receive a physical by the agency doctor before he leaves care. He'll be asked if he wants blood work done. When the test results come back Benny will sit with his eyes closed and his chin pressed to his chest.

He'll tell Bautista later that Marshall said not using a condom proved that what they had between them was special. Benny wanted so badly for that to be true he allowed himself to believe it. He will say he wanted to go down a different path from his mother's, but he guessed he couldn't scheme fate. His life has always been cursed. Why should it change now?

In the 401, the footsteps of the residents thunder overhead. I can hear them racing down the staircase.

"Slow down," Ms. Celeste calls out to the ceiling. "Somebody's going to break their neck on their own graduation day." The rumble of Montana and Benny racing down the staircase precedes them until they're pushing against each other in the doorway, panting. Montana is wearing her blue cap and gown. Benny is freshly showered, dressed in stiffly ironed shirt and slacks. He didn't hold back. On his face are his Dolce & Gabbana knockoff sunglasses. Both of his cellphones are holstered to his belt although the service was cut off months ago. He clips his collar between his thumb and forefinger, and then adjusts his cuffs with a quick throw of his shoulders. Their faces beam.

"Things are going to be good. I can feel it," Benny says and looks at Montana with a grin. "We going places, girl. Graduating is just the beginning. You feel me? We gonna make it. I feel it, yo. I really do. I can see us in the future. We gonna live the life, yo. We gonna live it."

CHAPTER 2

DRASTIC ESCAPES

The Incredible Hulk's fist is sticking out of a pile of rubble. Old issues of *Vibe* magazine are scattered everywhere. There's a lighter shaped like a woman. Her large breasts, when flicked, ignite a flame. Paperbacks are strewn all over, the covers torn off, the pages looking oxidized and burned around the edges. Boxer shorts litter the floor. Socks have fallen around the room like shell casings following a gunner in a war. And this mess does look like war. The kind that plays itself out inside someone's head, never meant for anyone to see but that becomes uncontainable, eventually spilling into the real world.

I'm on my hands and knees, positioned just outside Montana's closet door. I pick up the green fist, can't figure out what it's for, and toss it in the "maybe" pile. The magazines are just taking up space. They get thrown into a garbage bag. Two vinyl bags—"Puerto Rican rice bags," they're called here—are full of dirty laundry I pulled from around the room. The large bag in the corner is filled with trash collected from under her bed, and the "maybe" pile keeps growing. Like Montana, her stuff is stubborn. It doesn't want to be contained.

Downstairs, Montana is on the PlayStation. Since graduating high school a few weeks ago, this is where she hangs out. The faint sound of the game makes its way upstairs: gunshots, squealing car tires. I'm supposed to be helping *her* clean, but she became flustered as we searched through her belongings, scrutinizing each item's value. Was it worth keeping or not? If she thought it was, could she say why? Watching her things sifted through was too aggravating to bear. She stormed downstairs, so now I'm at it alone.

Residents are required to keep their rooms in order. It's a rule of the agency. Each morning their beds are to be made, their belongings stored and tidy. If they don't do it, it becomes my job. Montana's roommate, Sybella, keeps her side of the room up to code. Montana's side, in contrast, looks like layered sediment. When asked to clean, her solution has been to shove everything into her closet, sweep everything under the proverbial rug. That approach kept staff off her back for a while, but now the door to her closet won't shut.

The room carries the stale smell of adolescence and sleep. I have on the rubber gloves from the kitchen that stop just short of my elbows. I hold my breath as I dig my hand deep into the belly of the mess, pulling toward me crumpled-up notebook paper, empty Twizzler wrappers, old batteries, used Kleenex, and a coffee cup. The work sets off flurries of dust and debris. When given opportunities to clean the room herself, Montana balked, scoffing when told the state of her room could put the house in jeopardy if there was an inspection. Gena gave her plenty of chances. I was told today was it; her room had to be cleaned one way or another.

I hear movement at the door and look up to find Montana standing there, watching me.

"I'm going out," she says, surveying my progress. Her Mets cap tips slightly to the left, the bill just off center, the sale sticker reflecting the hallway light. "Just down the block," she says. I've learned that *down the block* is code for getting high. She walks over to the Incredible Hulk's fist, clenched and defiant, and picks it up. She eyes the pile I've made.

"What you doing with this?" she asks.

"It's in the 'maybe' pile."

Her face tightens.

"Maybe what?"

"Maybe it goes," I say. "It doesn't do anything, only adds to the mess."

She turns it over and shows me the knobs on the bottom of the Hulk's severed hand.

"It's a radio," she says.

"Well, it was at the bottom of your closet. You never use it. Plus you have a radio right there," I say, gesturing to a beat-up clock-radio resting on the cluttered bookshelf I have yet to tackle. Her eyes get smaller. I can see anger smoldering.

"Gena gave it to me for my birthday last year," she says firmly.

I'm not throwing anything out but she doesn't know that. I'm hoping she'll be pushed into participating in this cleanup if she thinks there's a chance something valuable will be lost. I'm just putting everything in her room in bags, organizing the clutter. She can sift through it all later if she wants.

"This is my stuff," she says, her voice rising.

"Exactly. If you help me, I'll know what's important and what isn't."

"You can't just throw my stuff away," she says. "There're rules." Now her voice breaks. "I'll sue."

Rules. Most residents grew up without them. At the 401, an agenda is set for each day. We try to map out all hours so that hardly anything is left to the imagination. Everything here is labeled and contained. Open the supply closet and you'll see an infantry of identical miniature shampoos, soaps, and detergents lined up for the taking. Individuality is lauded here, exemplified by handmade posters and affirming messages. But in reality individuality is difficult to practice, and that causes frustration among the youth.

My own rule is simple. Go to work. The more I do this job, the more engaged I become. I've turned all my focus to the tools of my new trade: the daily log where I have to document the happenings of each resident in the house; the progress and incident reports that get faxed to the main office; the missing persons reports that are completed and sent to the police when a resident is AWOL for more than twenty-four hours; the packet titled "Therapeutic Crisis Intervention" that's filled with acronyms meant to help me remember strategies for de-escalating conflicts; the arcane, old-fashioned food log. I spend long stretches of time writing, transcribing the residents' responses and interactions in the home, tracking a narrative. Knowing that what I've written may inform the administrative staff's decisions about how to proceed with a resident gives me a quiet satisfaction.

Getting lost in the storm of work at the 401 keeps me buoyed. I jump at the chance to pick up extra shifts. I stay late to help Ms. Celeste with the food order or chaperone a resident to a medical appointment. The needs here seem endless.

"If you followed the rules and kept your room clean in the first place we wouldn't be having this discussion," I say.

Montana reaches for a wrinkled McDonald's paper bag with a love poem scribbled on it. Her chin dimples. "My stuff ain't garbage," she says in a sharp tone, blinking back her frustration.

I gesture to the piles of newspapers, empty cigarette packs, bottles of Snapple, the syrupy and sticky surface of her nightstand. "Then help me," I say. "Let's do this together."

She looks at the overgrowth of her room, how unmanageable it all is, and her face twists. She disappears into the hallway. When I hear the front door slam shut behind her, I turn back to her closet and stare at the green fist. Like Bruce Banner transforming into the Incredible Hulk, Montana becomes helpless against the internal storm gathering force, never quite able to manage the ire swarming inside her.

"Most of them won't graduate from high school and can't hold down a job?" Ethan asks, looking at his BlackBerry. "Isn't that depressing? What's the point if there isn't any indication of success?"

I stab my straw into a tall glass of iced tea as our overpriced Cobb salads arrive at the table. Ethan, a friend from high school who now works as a public relations executive for a bank, is in New York on business and offered to take me out to lunch.

"The challenge of it, I guess. There isn't a high success rate but if I can help one kid, help them to see their potential, it's worth it." I think to tell him about Montana, the struggles she faces, but I don't. He probably doesn't care anyway. People prefer to ignore tragedy unless there's redemption in the end.

"That must be frustrating," he says.

"Of course, but rewarding," I say, looking down at my hands.

The restaurant he chose is in Midtown Manhattan and has high vaulted ceilings with a spare, minimalist design. The bar is an enormous, sleek slab of cherry wood. As we entered, the wait staff stood against the wall with their hands clasped in front of their aprons, dressed in crisp white shirts and offering saccharine smiles. I feel uncomfortable in my cut-offs, T-shirt, and flip-flops.

"If they just applied themselves, don't you think they could experience success like anyone else?" Ethan asks.

Before doing this work I carried some of the same misconceptions. I tell him about what I've learned on the job, about the obstacles facing LGBTQ youth in foster care, how many of them have experienced trauma and have little in the way of support. I tell him that these youth are at higher risk for all forms of maltreatment; that they experience more anxiety and depression; that they are more susceptible to drug abuse, homelessness, and violence than the general population. I say that living in poverty only exacerbates those issues.

Ethan picks through his salad as I natter on, telling him foster care feels like a prep course for incarceration in some ways, which is also disproportionately filled with people of color. Both systems warehouse people who have battled poverty and experienced unbalanced opportunities as well as systemic racism. I can't tell if Ethan's listening or lost in the hunt for a rogue slice of avocado. I become flustered but continue, pointing out that their lack of success is not about lack of ambition. The playing field is skewed. Our ability to attain an education, the luxury of choosing a career, and our lack of contentious run-ins with the law have more to do with our white, middle-class background than with motivation or choices.

Ethan stops eating and throws me a weighty stare. My idealism feels childish under the burden of his gaze. I clear my throat and look away. Lunch ends abruptly when he receives a text from his boss. They need to reconvene earlier than he had thought. We both reach for our wallets after he summons the waiter, but we both know, on my part, it's only a gesture.

"Lunch is on me," he says, sliding the check close to him.

"I need to talk to Tulip."

This is what her mother calls her. Tulip Montana. She phones the 401 daily. The first time I answered the phone I told her she had the wrong number, no Tulip lived here. Montana sprang up from the couch, clearly embarrassed, and said it was for her.

Initially I didn't notice anything strange about her mother's phone calls. Then they became more frequent until they were obsessive and disruptive. There are days when it seems like we can't go five minutes without a phone call from Montana's mother. When the calls become more neurotic, her voice is shrill, her words, rapid. Montana enters the office after I yell for her.

I hand the phone over and hear her mother say, "That lady is going to try to kidnap you again." Montana sits in Gena's desk chair, her forehead pressed against the wall. Her mother has bipolar disorder, or she's schizoaffective. The diagnosis always seems to change.

"No mom, Grandma isn't trying to take me," she says, her eyes closed. "No, Sybella is fine too."

When Montana was fourteen, her mother could no longer care for her, and she moved in with her grandmother. But her grandmother was getting older, and dealing with an adolescent was more than she could take. Montana's mother was in and out of psychiatric hospitals, and as Montana got older, her relationship with her daughter began to change. Initially she had no issue with Montana's sexuality, but as her mental health worsened and her fixation on church and the Bible grew, she became more critical of her daughter, until finally she claimed Montana was possessed by the devil and needed to be saved. Montana's grandmother, also religious albeit less extreme, found a way to accept her granddaughter for who she was. The difference in opinion left the two women estranged. Montana felt it was up to her to keep her grandmother and mother on speaking terms. She clung to the hope that she'd be able to keep her family together. It was a losing proposition, and being put into foster care caused her more stress than her young mind could manage.

Montana holds the receiver away from her ear and I can hear her mother's voice, reverberating as if she's calling from inside an echo chamber. "That demon is up to no good again. She killed my real family and kidnapped me when I was a baby. She's going to try to take you and kill me too, you just watch."

Montana's fingers tighten around the phone cord.

"Grandma's not going to try and kill nobody."

"That demon-lady is a trifling thing. You don't mess with God's affairs. She's evil, Tulip. Evil. You keep away from her. I'm gonna call my congressman on Monday and have that woman locked up."

"Mom, you're talking nonsense. Stop, please."

"Nonsense? She murdered my family and took me for her own. You call that nonsense? She'll do it again, Tulip."

Tears are beading down Montana's cheeks, collecting at her chin.

"Mom, you need to be on your meds. When you stop taking your meds?"

She doesn't wait for an answer and hangs up. She stares at nothing, lets out a breath. Just as I'm about to ask if she's OK, the phone rings again.

The following week Gena once more has me cleaning Montana's room. It's even more of a disaster this time than it was two weeks ago. Montana's become more despondent, pulling away from the program. She rarely talks to me or the other residents anymore, spending more and more time down the block.

I have on my requisite rubber gloves. Sweat drips down my face. I wipe it away with my forearm and scan Montana's room for a moment. After spending hours cleaning, I have made a line against the wall of bloated garbage bags filled with her belongings. Her dresser and nightstand are dusted, the floor vacuumed, her bed made. Both sides of the room are now distinguishable only by Sybella's stuffed animal collection and Montana's assortment of baseball caps. For the sake of appearances, her room is clean, made to look like everyone else's. If the city were to surprise us with one of its random inspections, we'd pass. Ms. Celeste had warned that if rooms weren't clean, the city could shut us down. But it's not something we need to consider today. The room is orderly, therefore the resident must be fine, the reasoning goes.

I'm still on the floor when Montana enters, flapping the bottom of her basketball jersey to cool herself off. She ogles me crouched down, my hand inside her bottom dresser drawer. "What the fuck you doing?" she asks.

I stand, dust off my knees. "You let things go again. Gena told me to clean up."

Her nostrils flare. "You can't keep going through my shit."

"I'm just doing my job, Montana."

She walks over to the nightstand and looks back to me. "Where's my journal? And what'd you do with the letter I put here?"

She grunts and swipes at her lamp, causing it to crash to the ground. "This shit is so fucked up."

I clamber for a response, trying to remember the training materials, the acronyms outlining crisis intervention. When a situation escalates, I'm to explore the resident's point of view. "This must be frustrating for you," I say. "You know I'm willing to help you organize next time."

She searches my face for a moment. "Are you fucking kidding me?" she asks. She rips down her work uniform hanging from the closet door and rushes down the stairs. I look at the bags filled with her belongings. The sense of accomplishment I felt moments ago is undermined by knowing that Montana sees this for what it is: a radical invasion of privacy. I'm afraid she thinks I'm trying to pry apart her personality, seize possession of it, pack it in bags, and keep it out of sight.

When I started at the 401 Montana was the one resident everyone deemed to have the most potential. She went to class regularly, then graduated high school, maintained employment, and did her chores. Each morning she'd wake up early, grab one of the coveted sugar cereals from the family packs in the cupboard (if there were any left), snatch the newspaper from the stoop, and read about the world while spooning trinket-shaped marshmallows into her mouth. She was quick to share her opinions with me on the president's policies, the NYPD, the war in Iraq, all before most of the residents had even stepped out of bed. I tried to introduce her to NPR's *Morning Edition,* but she preferred the paper. Those "white people's voices made me mad sleepy," she said.

I was happy to have someone in the house who followed current events. Most of the residents showed no interest in what was happening outside of themselves; their own traumas seemed to eclipse their empathy for others. When I tried to talk with Benny about the handling of prisoners at Abu Ghraib, he shot back, "So the fuck what? Rikers any different?" Sybella feigned astonishment at the news of the Sudanese genocide, but it was clear that the place seemed too abstract, too foreign for those people to be real. Reginald hadn't even heard that a gay marriage bill had passed in Massachusetts and seemed entirely unaffected by the idea. Gay couples who considered marriage were mostly white and upper-middle class, and way outside his scope of experience.

But Montana was different. Despite her own struggles—growing up in abject poverty, always on the verge of homelessness, having a mother struggling with severe mental illness, and facing rejection when coming to terms with her own sexual identity—she was engaged with the world around her. I cherished my mornings with her, even if we both only studied the paper silently. They started my day off well and served as a reminder, when things began to blow off course in the house, that there was something sturdy to return to.

Two nights a week Montana works as a security guard in Manhattan. She dons her oversized navy sport coat, white button-down shirt, and gray slacks. She hasn't learned how to tie a tie, so it remains in a slack knot that can be adjusted in the collar of her shirt. I've learned that her mother hasn't been able to secure employment because of her refusal to consistently take her medication. Despite never having had an adult in her life to model her work ethic after, Montana takes it upon herself to bring in the menial income her job provides.

Security jobs are popular among group home residents. The pay is minimal but it doesn't require a complex skill set. Chances for advancement are slim besides a slight pay increase if you last long enough. Other entry-level jobs like at McDonald's or Dunkin' Donuts are labor-intensive in comparison and require some customer service skills. It's assumed that most of the residents wouldn't last long. If it wasn't the work itself that would set them off, it'd be taking direction from the manager or relenting to a demanding customer. At least with security the only thing to battle against is boredom.

When I tell Gena that I think Montana's potential is being minimized, she gives me a knowing nod. Yes, Montana is considered high-functioning in the group home, but in the outside world she becomes confused, obstinate.

"We've tried her at other jobs and she always ends up getting fired," Gena says.

I'm hopeful that she'll be able to build toward working at Starbucks after leaving foster care, where she'd qualify for health insurance benefits if she can handle the minimum of working twenty hours a week. Most of the residents, even some of the highest-functioning ones, aren't able to manage at that level. So they remain in jobs like security, where they have little contact with the outside world and little chance to mess up.

It's nighttime. I wait as the other residents go upstairs and get ready for bed. This is the first time Montana hasn't come home by curfew. She should have been here an hour ago, after her shift ended. I listen to Benny and Rodrigo above me arguing over who gets to use the bathroom first as I absentmindedly flip the key ring at my side, glancing every so often at the front door. It's been a quiet evening. No obstinate behavior, no fights or freakouts. The other residents finished their chores without incident. Not showing up after work is completely out of character for Montana, and for me, it is cause for alarm. The other residents don't seem to pay it any mind. When I asked Sybella where she thought Montana could be, she shrugged. Her eyes were heavy from a long day of school, followed by night school. She carried herself up the stairs to her room to prepare for tomorrow morning, when she has to do it all over again. "Don't know," she said, dragging her book bag behind her. "Probably down the block with Unique."

Unique is a middle-aged man who hangs out with the teenagers in the neighborhood. He's rumored to be a pimp but the residents deny it, pointing out that he runs his own business. Unique has seemingly parlayed his neighborhood bully status into a career. All around the area his handmade signs are tacked up to light poles and bus stops. They read, "Unique Security: We Bust Heads."

At eleven o'clock I shut the house down, flip off the lights, and activate the alarm system. If Montana comes home, she'll have to ring the doorbell to be let in. If she doesn't come home I'll have to call the police in the morning and file a missing person's report. In the office I write in the logbook. "House is secure. All residents accounted for except for Montana."

I'm startled by a knock on the front door. When I go to unlock it, I see Montana standing with her baseball cap pulled low. She tries to get past me without saying anything.

"It's an hour past curfew," I say and block the doorway with my arm.

She keeps her chin tucked to her chest. The musky-sweet odor of marijuana wafts from her clothes. She pushes again toward the steps leading to her room.

"Wait a minute," I say, positioning myself between her and the staircase. I try to get a look at her face. Her eyes are beady and red. "What's going on? Are you all right?"

She doesn't respond. When I ask if she's high, she looks up indignantly.

"I ain't gonna front. I'm faded. You got something to say about it?"

Her haughtiness reminds me of my own responses to my parents when I came home late, high, and full of arrogance.

"I'm concerned about you, Montana."

She scoffs, then stares blindly at the floor.

"You only care 'cause you're paid to."

When I say that that isn't true, something seems to unhinge in her. She sucks in a quivering breath, then unleashes a diatribe about our program's failures. The youth in this house need structure, she says, but staff don't do shit. No one is held accountable for anything, then staff expect them to just get up and move out on their twenty-first birthday. This place is fucking useless, she argues.

I look at her. There's a tense silence between us as I search her face. "What happened today?"

Her eyes close tight, and she seems to hold her breath until she shoots me a cold glance.

"I got fired, OK? So I went to chill down the block, blow off some steam," she says, maneuvering around me. "Now leave me the fuck alone."

The administrative staff hold weekly meetings where we discuss the progress of each resident. This week a disproportionate amount of time is spent talking about Montana. Jessica, Laura, and Steve—Montana's caseworker—sit along with Gena, Ms. Celeste, and me in a semicircle in the office. The recent change in Montana's behavior has everyone worried. Gena gets us up to date on Montana's antisocial behavior in the house, how she spends more and more time out of the home, how she refuses to follow most of the agency's rules and regulations, how she lost her job because she was caught smoking pot. There's concern that she's working for Unique now, in what capacity, no one knows. The most recent development is that Montana told Ms. Celeste she wants to sign herself out of care and move back in with her mother. She said she's had enough of everyone meddling in her business. As I hear this, I can't help feeling she's talking about me.

"Only a month ago she graduated high school, had a job, and was considering community college," Jessica says. "She's regressing rapidly."

Montana's sudden desire to leave the program and live with her mother doesn't surprise me. She seems to be looking for any type of drastic escape to pull her from the mire of her current situation. Just last week she broke her typical depressive sluggishness when she received a letter from a writing foundation where she'd submitted a poem. The foundation claimed she'd won an award. Ten thousand dollars. She waved the letter around, her face flush with relief. Finally, she'd be free from the circumstances fettering her. I scanned the paper, the official-looking letterhead, skeptical of any organization claiming to hand out hefty prizes for anguished teen poetry. Sure enough, the fine print explained she'd be considered for the grand prize after sending in a subscription fee of five hundred dollars. When I gently pointed this out, Montana's face dropped, then filled with color, her eyes unable to hold back the tears building until they streamed down her cheeks. "Jesus, Ryan," she said and collapsed onto the couch, her chest heaving. I couldn't help but feel I'd crushed what little hope she had left.

I mention her interest in writing and current events to the group. Maybe getting her to focus on her talents will help her regain direction in her life? I tell everyone I know of a writer's workshop for students that might suit her well.

"This child needs to learn life skills, not how to be a poet," Ms. Celeste says. "There's nothing wrong with doing unskilled labor. It's what she's capable of right now. Filling these kids' heads with distractions is a disservice."

I smile weakly and nod.

Laura says Montana has refused to continue therapy with her. She then reminds us that depression can be triggered by all types of life events, not only humiliation, failure, or loss. This might explain Montana's lack of drive, she says, and her inability to organize herself. She's the first person in her family to graduate high school. Now that this goal has been met she seems unsure where to go, what to do, who she is. Montana has always seen herself as the glue keeping her family together. But much of their contention is due to her sexuality, and I suspect she blames herself for being placed in foster care. Her success in school coupled with her perceived failure to mend family wounds may have created a confusion that pushed her off a cliff.

Two weeks have passed since our last incident in her room and Montana is sitting on the couch with her feet propped up on the coffee table, obsessing about an article she's read in the newspaper. This is what she does now. This week's topic is murder/suicide. A three-year-old boy in the Lower East Side found his mother strangled to death, nylon tied around her neck by his father. The man dangled from a rope a few feet away. The boy went next door to his aunt's apartment and told her, "My mommy and daddy are dead."

Montana still has vague plans to move out. When I ask her about her intentions, she ignores me and instead recalls details of the article she's reading. The couple seemed fine. A few arguments, but by all appearances everything seemed fine. The woman's aunt said the mother never mentioned any problems but she could tell something was wrong because of her silence.

"That shit's crazy," Montana says, and tears the article out of the newspaper. "How you going to leave that little kid an orphan?"

The administrative staff believes her depression is worsening, but Montana refuses to address it. She's still skipping therapy with Laura, retreating farther and farther into herself, snubbing all efforts the agency has made to provide help. Now that she's jobless Montana is supposed to spend her days searching for work; instead she spends most of her time sleeping, getting high, or obsessing over newspaper articles. Lately, the only time she talks in the house is when discussing a news story. She seems to find a way into her own life through the accounts of strangers. Other people's stories allow her to understand her own.

I descend into the dark stairwell leading to Montana's mother's basement apartment. The steps are cluttered with old bathrobes, dusty boots, and stoop-sale paintings. In the bathroom, extension cords and hair dryers hang like spider legs. Towels are piled on the tile floor. Montana is in the living room sitting on a sectional couch, blindly staring at the television. The newscaster is talking about a police shooting in New York. The victim was unarmed. His mother's only child.

Around her are tipped cereal boxes. Marshmallow trinkets collect in the crevices of the couch. Clothes cover the backs of chairs, clump in piles on the floor. Cardboard boxes are stacked all over the room. The blinds are drawn, leaving the room cast in a shadowy gloom.

"Montana," I say. "It's time."

Her mother called the 401 that morning, insisting we pick up her daughter. In little over a week, she determined they couldn't live together. It was too much to handle. I look at Montana, her face expressionless and numb, and wonder if she's scared she'll end up like her mother. I wonder if she's been on the lookout for the signs in herself she witnesses when they're together: the increased paranoia, loss of ambition, irritability. Perhaps she's trying to find a cure by self-medicating with her daily blunt.

I grab her backpack from the couch and hoist it onto my shoulder.

"How they going to take that child from his mother," she mutters. Her eyes never leave the screen.

Her mother has shut herself in her bedroom, unable to face the failure of their reunion. Gradually Montana gets up, still entranced by what's on the screen. She stretches her arms overhead then wiggles her feet into her shoes. She's talking again about the police shooting, that child who was ripped from his mother's life.

I say goodbye as we pass the closed bedroom door, but there's no response. Montana keeps her head low, pulls the bill of her cap toward her nose. We make our way up the stairs and out into the bright summer day. She walks toward the van, then pauses a moment. She looks back at the dilapidated door of the apartment, then turns around and heads back into her mother's chaos, disappearing inside. Moments later Montana re-emerges into the daylight, cradling the Incredible Hulk fist-radio as delicately as if it were her child. I start up the van and try to smile as she climbs in.

CHAPTER 3

TICK TICK BOOM

Every few days or so, when his loneliness becomes impossible to bear, Rodrigo leaves his Manhattan high school and goes to Central Park. He wanders off the paved roads and makes his way to the secluded, wooded trails, just a few blocks from the housing project in Harlem where he grew up. There, he drifts and waits. He might lean against a tree or roam along a trail. Eventually a man will show up. He'll be older than Rodrigo, sometimes as old as his father. They'll stare at each other for too long without looking away. Then the man will ramble deeper into the woods, looking back to see if Rodrigo will follow. And he will. Most of the men want Rodrigo to crouch down in front of them, unzip their flies, but on rare occasions a man will want to service him. I imagine Rodrigo tilting his head back, staring at the clouds, trying hard not to look at the skyscrapers on the fringe of this dream, which would pull him back into reality. I imagine he wants to stay here, away from the noise of his life, away from how complicated everything has become. I imagine that he concentrates on the warmth enveloping him, on the clouds overhead that move and change and meld together. I imagine Rodrigo shares himself with this man, with any man he meets in the park, because he's thankful for the attention, offering whatever it is the man may want, hoping something elemental will be exchanged. Hoping this will make him feel whole.

I can hear the sound from the TV wafting in from the living room. It's Wednesday night, which means *America's Next Top Model* is on. Watching it has become a ritual at the 401, but tonight Rodrigo needs to talk to me. So here we are, in the office with the purring fluorescent lights. Typically it's his family or his struggles to fit in that he wants to discuss. I'm taken by surprise when he mentions cruising the park, and I try to swallow the embarrassment rising inside me.

"How long have you been going there?" I ask.

Rodrigo pauses for a moment to adjust the choker around his neck, then kicks the carpet with his combat boots. A metal-studded belt cinches his plaid shorts. He smiles, his spirited eyes reduced to slits.

"A while. Since I was twelve, maybe. I used to cut class and go to the park to draw." He leans toward me. "I didn't know what I was about to get into." He pauses, his smile widening. "Or maybe I did."

My throat constricts, but I try to appear measured. As a residential counselor, I should be beyond the discomfort that the residents bring up in me. I'm not. Rodrigo tells me about his first threesome while I cross my arms over my chest. I'm not clinically trained; I've made that clear to him. Still, he's asked if I can replace Laura and become his therapist. He confides in me because I'm the only staff member at the group home who tolerates his constant chatter. Because I'm just a residential counselor, I can't promise that what he tells me will be kept confidential. If he discloses something that compromises his well-being, I'm obligated to notify the administrative staff, and he knows it.

"Since then," he says, "it's like I can't stop. I'd be there all the time if I could." He laughs and shakes his head as if amazed by his own boldness.

Despite all of Rodrigo's outward rebellion, he exudes a heartbreaking naïveté. Although he grew up in the projects, he's never become streetwise. Watching him fold one leg under himself and clasp his hands in his lap, I can't help but see his contradictions. The spikes and chains and torn T-shirts are in contrast to his soft eyes and sensitive face. His revolt seems mostly cosmetic. He lacks the anger of his fellow housemates.

The other Latino residents at the group home don't like Rodrigo. "Where your Boricua gene?" Caridad asked him once, to which Benny replied, "*No tiene na.'* His moms didn't feed him enough *arroz con gandules y costillitas.*" Benny continues, "He looks all *cochino,*" pointing out Rodrigo's sleeveless Misfits T-shirt, his ripped jeans clad with safety pins, his unshaven face. I've learned that when you come from the projects, appearing wealthy is nearly as important as having money. No one in the house gets why Rodrigo dresses so sloppily. The black residents call him "grimy" to his face. He's an outcast, even in this group home of outcasts, and maybe because of this I'm drawn to him.

"You ever been?" he asks me.

"What?"

He laughs a goofy laugh that reminds me he is only seventeen. "The park." He says it like he's talking about carousels, jungle gyms. "There a lot of white dudes like you there."

I get up and pretend to adjust the air conditioner. I hear the muffled sounds of *America's Next Top Model* and wish I were sitting on the couch with the other residents.

"Cruising in parks is dangerous, Rodrigo. Especially for someone your age," I say.

He nods. "I know."

"If you know, why do you do it?"

Rodrigo spreads his arm out on the desk next to him, rests his head on it, and stares dreamily. "Go to the park?" he asks, scratching at his purple-dyed hair with his free hand, then rubbing the bridge of his nose, leaving a smudge. "Because I know I'm always going to find somebody who wants me."

Rodrigo's mother rarely leaves the couch in her dark apartment. He tells me she watches telenovelas all day. Both she and his older sister are diagnosed schizophrenics and receive monthly disability checks that support the whole family. In the neighborhood they are the subject of myths and ridicule. When Rodrigo's older brother, John, lost their dog, a rumor began to circulate that their mother had boiled it and served it with fried plantains because she'd run out of food stamps. To walk into their house, the story went, was to wade through a sea of garbage and animal feces. When Rodrigo lived at home, the bullies that John regularly hung out with tormented him about his beat-up Converse sneakers, plaid pants, and feminine swagger. "*Puto sucio!*" They'd shout. Dirty faggot. "*Tu hueles como basura.*" You smell like garbage.

John rose above the rumors by proving himself as a drug runner. Rodrigo and his little brother, Josef, rarely attended school, showing up only occasionally for free breakfast and lunch. Rodrigo told me that when he was younger, his father had made rules about chores and school, but he wasn't around to enforce them. Everyone knew their father had moved in with a second family in Brooklyn. He had kids with his new wife and had given them the same names as Rodrigo and his siblings.

Rodrigo said he felt his father was ashamed of them and was giving himself a "do over," periodically drifting up to Harlem to collect money from the disability checks, then disappearing again.

As oldest male, John became the unofficial head of the house. He stopped defending Rodrigo from other kids on the street and told him to toughen up. He wasn't going to look out for Rodrigo forever. John started seeing a girl down the block and spending less time at home.

Whenever his brothers come up in our conversations, Rodrigo's cheeks flush, and his eyes stare at nothing. According to Rodrigo, everything started to fall apart when his brother didn't want him to come out of the closet to his family. John brought girls over to the apartment and tried to persuade Rodrigo to sleep with them, even offered him money if he did. But Rodrigo came out anyway. When John announced he was moving out to live with his new girlfriend, Rodrigo felt he was abandoning their family, just like their father had. The brothers began arguing one day, not realizing their mother's social worker was in the next room for a home inspection. They fought, and John landed a punch square on his brother's nose. Blood poured out as John held Rodrigo down and told him to stop acting like such a "faggot."

Their mother and the social worker entered the bedroom. That's when Rodrigo said it, right there in front of everybody.

"I said, 'If I'm all faggot, what that make you?' I told him he was the one who made me like that. How he going to call me a faggot when he the one doing it to me?"

John began to protest as the social worker pulled out her notebook and started writing. All their mother said was, "Stop bleeding on my floor. I got my social worker here." Rodrigo was taken from his home and isn't allowed to set foot in his mother's apartment unsupervised until he turns eighteen.

I'm still working one night a week at the Mexican restaurant because my checks from the group home barely pay the rent. Tonight after my shift I sit at the bar. Dan, a regular, slouches on his stool next to me, his fat fingers toying with my pack of cigarettes before he asks to bum one. His eyes are red, their lids heavy. He rubs his unshaven cheek, and I think how he looks older than he is. I wonder if I look the same. He lights the cigarette, ignoring the city's smoking ban, and asks me about the group home.

Rodrigo comes to mind. Just before I left the 401 this week, he told me he had to go to court to testify to a judge about how he'd been molested for years by his brother John.

"You nervous?" I asked him.

"Yeah," he said. "My mom told me to drop it. She scared." He needed to be reassured that he was doing the right thing, but I didn't know what to say. I pulled him close and patted his shoulder, softly offering, "You'll be OK."

But I don't tell Dan about Rodrigo. Instead I talk about a harmless public meltdown Benny had last week at Jamaica Center when we didn't see the movie he wanted. For now, I keep Rodrigo to myself.

When I return to the 401 the following week, everything is in chaos. Montana has been fired from her job as a security guard because she was caught smoking weed. Sybella has stopped going to night school. Caridad, who's been AWOL, showed up high last night at 4:00 a.m. And Benny seems to have developed a Napoleon complex, not allowing anyone to use the phone or the TV without his permission. By the time I get around to Rodrigo, I can tell something's happened. He has trouble making eye contact and is high-strung. Earlier he snapped at Sybella when she tried to talk to him about organizing their joint birthday party. We sit together in the office, and he seems preoccupied. He wants to talk only about a man he's met at the local gay and lesbian community center.

"He just my type," Rodrigo says, followed by a stream of giggles. "He got a goatee."

Gena suggested that Rodrigo check out the community center. They have an after-school program that offers art and music classes and gives LGBTQ youth a safe place to socialize. The administrative staff in our program had tried other ways of engaging Rodrigo in less self-destructive activities. There was a short-lived mentoring program where residents were matched with adults in the community. Most of the mentors were unprepared to deal with the struggles the residents had. We canceled Rodrigo's mentorship after he decided to sunbathe in transparent briefs with his mentor when they went to the beach.

Rodrigo tells me that the man with the goatee operates a food cart. Rodrigo's leg hammers up and down as he plays with the Wite-Out on Gena's desk, unscrewing the top and taking a quick sniff. "I told him he should invite me over to his crib after he finish work." Rodrigo starts painting his thumbnail with the Wite-Out.

"You know that's not a good idea."

Rodrigo looks up, thinking I'm talking about decorating his nails.

"You don't know anything about this guy," I say. "Don't you think he's too old for you?" He goes back to finishing off his thumbnail. I try to find out what he likes about the guy, but all Rodrigo will say is that he has a goatee. So I steer the conversation away and ask if Rodrigo has been in contact with his father. He puts the Wite-Out down, and something in his face hardens. "He back in Puerto Rico."

"You told me he lives in Brooklyn with a second family."

"Well, he got ghost when he heard I got put up in here."

I ask why his father would move; Rodrigo shrugs. I can tell the conversation is making him uncomfortable, but I don't stop prying. Something is being left out.

Rodrigo wraps his arms around his belly, glowers. "We almost done?"

I lean back in my chair. "Yeah, of course."

He gets up to leave.

"You're OK, though?"

Rodrigo nods but doesn't look up as he walks out the door.

The residents are huddled around the TV, watching *America's Next Top Model*. I'm sitting at the edge of the room on a chair I've pulled from the dinner table. Everyone stares at the screen with rapt attention—everyone except Rodrigo, who's pacing the periphery, his fingers flicking near his ears. He pauses, cocks his head. One hand covers his mouth, and he mutters something to himself. Montana and Sybella seem to have blocked him out, but Benny, I can tell, is annoyed. As Rodrigo begins to lap the room again, Benny blurts out, "What the fuck is your problem?"

"Watch the show," Montana says to Rodrigo.

"*Watch the show*," Rodrigo mimics, then begins to laugh. It's a hollow, artificial laugh that goes on for too long.

The residents begin talking about Rodrigo as if he's not there until Benny's eyes narrow.

"How they going to put these crazy motherfuckers in here with us? You know one night he going to crack and pull some *Friday the 13th* type shit," he says. Benny leans toward Rodrigo. "Hey, don't go chopping nobody into little pieces when they sleeping, yo."

The other residents laugh and so does Rodrigo. Then his face turns stony. Then he laughs again, starting to howl, clutching his gut, red-faced, bending over. I've decided not to jump in just yet. I'm hoping the residents can work out this dispute on their own.

"Fucking freak," Benny says, turning back to the show. "People be treating you better if you stop being so backwards."

This prompts Rodrigo to run up to the TV with exaggerated, faux curiosity. He looks back at the other residents and pretends to bite his nails. "Oh, my God, who they going to vote off tonight? The anticipation is killing me!"

"Shut the fuck up, bitch," Benny says, sitting up, his shoulders tight. The room feels tense.

Rodrigo rushes over to him, stopping just short of colliding with his legs. "You mad funny!" Rodrigo screams, only inches from Benny's face.

I get up. Benny turns to me, his fists clenched. "This punk better get outta my face, or I'ma make him get outta my face," he says to me. I wedge between them, bring Rodrigo into the office, and shut the door. He plops down and smiles so big his eyes are hidden behind mounds of cheek. I ask him if he thinks this is funny and warn him that one day he's going to push someone too far and get punched.

"Good."

I stare at him until we're both uncomfortable. "What's going on? This isn't like you."

He shrugs and says he was just playing. He picks at the scabs around his wrist left by a too-tight leather wristband. If he's feeling anxious, I tell him, he needs to talk to a staff member or his therapist. Rodrigo mouths, "OK," his fingers now interlaced in his lap.

I get up, ask him to apologize to his housemates, then pat him on the shoulder, indicating he's free to go. Rodrigo nods and gives me a smile that says, "I'm sorry," then goes back to the living room.

I open the logbook and start writing up the incident. Rodrigo will probably get a "level drop" because of this, ending five weeks of continued success. Often a change in status can send a resident into a streak of bad behavior. I write that I think we need to keep Rodrigo focused on his positive accomplishments. I want him to know he has a confidant in the house. I want to tell him I know what it's like to feel alienated, different.

A noise comes from down the hall. Then a scream.

"Fucking freak!" Benny yells.

I run into the living room to find Benny on top of Rodrigo, one hand around his throat, the other reared back in a fist.

Rodrigo's lips are moving, saying something over and over that I can't make out. Not until I get close enough to separate them can I tell that he's pleading with Benny.

"Please," he begs. "Hit me."

A few days later, I'm putting out extra folding chairs in the office, setting out soda and bottled water and individual bags of chips. Rodrigo's caseworker, Steve, is meeting with Jessica, Gena, and Laura, to discuss the incident with Benny. Steve informs the group that Rodrigo's behavior was a result of what had happened at his hearing with the judge earlier in the week. He didn't realize the repercussions of his allegations against his brother. John is now nineteen years old, so a criminal case will be mounted. If convicted, his brother will go to prison. Rodrigo returned to the group home frightened and confused. Steve, overburdened with eleven other cases, forgot to inform the staff at the 401 of the outcome.

As a result of the incident, Steve says, Rodrigo had to undergo a psychiatric evaluation and was prescribed Risperdal.

"Risperdal?" I ask.

"An antipsychotic."

My colleagues scribble in their notebooks. No one seems troubled by this news. Maybe they're desensitized to this type of outcome. My throat tightens. I'm irritated with this overlit room and Steve's shrill voice. The clinical words only dance around Rodrigo's pain.

"Medicating him seems like a drastic response to the situation, don't you think?" I ask.

The scribbling stops. I suggest that Rodrigo's acting out was a cry for help. He felt overwhelmed by what he'd heard at court. I don't mention that he probably also felt let down by the program's failure to provide support. Aggravating Benny was his way to eclipse the pain he was feeling.

Jessica gives me a knowing look. "No one wants to medicate the residents unnecessarily," she says. "This is a doctor's diagnosis."

I'm told to continue my talks with Rodrigo because he trusts me. Jessica reminds me that I'm not a trained clinician. The talks are to remain casual and should not attempt to simulate a therapeutic environment. I need to keep the team informed of what we discuss.

The concern I've raised has been passed over, and the conversation moves on. It becomes clear that a diagnosis—even a possible misdiagnosis—reads as due diligence to the powers that be.

For the joint birthday party I've decorated the back-yard with pink and blue streamers and balloons. There isn't much to tack them onto, so the dented grill gets dressed up the most. Gena has bought the cakes—chocolate for Sybella, vanilla for Rodrigo—and had the first decorated with musical notes, the second with comic-book characters. I've ordered four cases of Pepsi, not the generic soda we normally have. Rodrigo is dressed in bas-ketball pants that snap up the side and a long-sleeve gray T-shirt. His hair is shaggy, the copper from his recent peroxide job already growing out, the black roots emerg-ing. He slogs around the backyard, occasionally sipping from his plastic cup of Pepsi, alone at his own party. The other residents have shunned him completely since the incident, calling him Tick Tick Boom. He ends up over by the tool shed, kicking at some mulch. I offer him a slice of his birthday cake, but he refuses. Not until the program van pulls into the driveway, the horn honking, does he perk up.

The side door opens, and Rodrigo's mother gets out. His sister, holding her toddler, lumbers behind. Josef fol-lows but doesn't stray far from the van. Benny puts on a CD, and Sybella and her best friend dance on the lawn. Rodrigo's sister sets down her toddler, who stumbles through the tall grass after a stray balloon. I try to intro-duce myself to Rodrigo's mother, but she won't look up from her plate. Gena walks over, toting a case of Pepsi under her arm and scanning the lawn full of teenagers.

"Where is Rodrigo?" she asks.

Inside, the living room is cool and quiet. Rodrigo and Josef are sitting on the love seat, away from the crowd. When I sit down on the arm of the chair next to them, they grow silent. I ask Josef if he'll be in high school this fall, and he seems to recoil from my words. There's no eye contact, not even a hint of a smile. Josef still lives with his mother because he's refused to corroborate Rodrigo's story. According to Steve, Josef said Rodrigo had lied, that John had never touched either of them.

"Wanna see something?" Rodrigo asks me.

He pulls a picture from his pocket and says Josef gave it to him for his birthday. In it a young man stands with his arm around a woman holding a baby, but the woman and child are hidden under Rodrigo's thumb. "That's John," he says of the man, who stands with long brown hair and a goatee.

Rodrigo's mother becomes restless after we give him his gifts, and she abruptly asks to be taken home. With petty cash we got him a book about how to draw comics and a new sketchpad. All the staff signed the card. When he showed his mother, embarrassment flashed across her face, and Rodrigo's momentary joy faded. I suddenly felt guilty for giving him the present in front of his mother, knowing she was unable to afford one.

Gena asks me to drive the family back to Harlem. In the van Rodrigo's mother sits in the passenger seat and stares silently out the window. As I drive across the Queensboro Bridge toward Manhattan, I occasionally look in my rearview mirror to find Josef resting his head in Rodrigo's lap. Rodrigo runs his fingers through his brother's hair and brushes his cheek with the back of his hand. They whisper to each other, softly laughing. I drop Rodrigo's family off, and he and I make our way back to Queens. He is quiet. The sun has just set, the last orange and plum streaks of daylight stretching out from the horizon. He flips on the radio, searches the stations, then turns it off.

"Eighteen years old," I say and reach over to pat his back. This is a big year, I tell him. He's going to graduate from high school, maybe take more art classes at the center. He's making healthier choices, not cruising the park anymore.

"No, I been there," Rodrigo says. "Every day this week." He stares out at the highway.

"Oh," I say. "I thought you were trying to stop that."

Rodrigo says he changed his mind and tells me about Rodney, a guy he met deep in the park. After having sex, they decided to offer older men blow jobs for twenty dollars.

Rodrigo pauses as if waiting for a reaction. I ask if he did it, and he says Rodney did once, but he was there. Things got out of control quickly. The man was larger than them and became aggressive. Before Rodrigo knew what was happening, Rodney pulled out a knife and screamed for the man to hand over his cash. The man threw them his money but said he was going to catch them and skin them alive. Scared, Rodrigo scrambled away.

I ask if anyone was hurt. When he answers no, I'm relieved.

"What the hell is going on?" I ask.

He's looking out the side window, but I can tell he's crying. "I don't know," he says, wiping his eyes with his wrist. "Sometimes it's like I can't feel nothing unless I do something crazy."

He becomes so still, I don't know what to do. I can't imagine being that young, so brutally violated by a family member, and having no one offer support. Maybe after a while he thought he deserved it. Maybe he thought his brother molested him because he wasn't man enough. I imagine Rodrigo becoming so plagued by the silence around his assault that he resolved never to open up about anything again, deciding never to show vulnerability, to compensate by acting out. Now he goes on resurrecting the anguish, seeking out the missing response.

Rodrigo begs me not to say anything to Gena or anyone else in the program. He feels guilty about what happened in the park. It won't happen again, he assures me. He just needed to get it off his chest. He asks me to promise not to tell anyone. I don't move my eyes from the road.

His voice cracks from crying. "Please," he says. "Promise."

A long silence builds up between us. I want to tell him that I know what it's like—the search for something outside himself to make him feel whole.

"OK," I say. "I promise." A deep regret fills me as soon as the words leave my mouth.

Back at the group home, I pace alone in the office. I want to slink away, not deal with the inevitable fallout from Rodrigo's confession. Instead, I sit down at Gena's desk and take the program phone directory from the top drawer of the filing cabinet. I find the extension I'm looking for and glance up to make sure there's no one outside the door. My voice is hushed as I leave a message on Steve's voicemail.

A week later, when it's time for Rodrigo's service-plan review, Gena asks me to be the representative from the 401. I'm supposed to talk about how he's adjusted to the program. I've been given a questionnaire to fill out, rating him on his willingness to follow rules: 1 indicating low functionality; 5, high functionality.

Rodrigo is sitting at the head of the table, flanked by his mother and Steve. Jessica is there. Gena too. The case manager from the Administration for Children's Services rushes in late, wearing a suit and tie, wrapping up a call on his cellphone. Many youth don't bother attending these meetings. I commend Rodrigo for showing up. For the next forty-five minutes he listens to us tell his life story. Steve says that, despite his long absence from school before entering foster care, his teachers report that he's catching up. If he continues at this pace, he'll be able to graduate with his class. The independent-living specialist talks about Rodrigo's art classes and his participation in the center's youth program. There's discussion about part-time employment or an internship. I talk about his willingness to bathe regularly, keep his room tidy, and socialize. Rodrigo follows rules well, I say, and is likable when he's not provoking the other residents. I mention his successes and a few stumbles along the way. Looking over at Rodrigo, I say that he has a lot of potential.

Steve concludes the meeting by stating the agency's goals for Rodrigo over the next six months: graduation, more art classes, and a part-time job. Just as it seems we're done, Steve says, "We have one more order of business to discuss." He looks at Rodrigo. "I hear you've been busy in the park again."

Rodrigo's eyes are fixed on the table in front of him. The room quiets.

"With all this success, why do you go to the park and have sex with strangers? You're putting your life at risk. You know that, don't you?"

Rodrigo nods slightly. His mother's face is expressionless.

"And I heard that this time you were asking for money. You have too much going for you to start prostituting."

Rodrigo glances up at me. I can't meet his eyes; instead I scan the questionnaire. The numbers that are meant to approximate his ability to live a successful life.

Steve tells him he's going to be put on "alarm," then continues to talk about the park. "Is that the life you want to live?" he asks.

"No," Rodrigo whispers.

The van sputters as it idles. Rodrigo and I sit silently, looking at his neighborhood. Boys in oversized T-shirts and drooping jeans gather on the courtyard benches, where Styrofoam Chinese takeout containers have been tossed to the pavement. Two mothers who look younger than Rodrigo prop their babies on their hips and lean against an abandoned Buick. Reggaeton music blasts and Puerto Rican flags flap from open apartment windows. I don't want Rodrigo to get out of the van. He's about to take a course of action that could destroy any chance he has at a moderately healthy life. Two days after his review he announced that he'd decided to sign himself out of care. He claimed it had nothing to do with the review. He needed to be back with his family. Rodrigo showed me the letter he'd written the judge, to clear up this mess he'd created.

"I made it all up," he said boldly. "John never touched me." In the letter he confessed that he'd only said it to get revenge against his brother for abandoning the family.

I drum my fingers on the steering wheel and watch two boys in the courtyard sneak up behind a girl, pour a drink on her, and run. I'm wary of Rodrigo's sudden reversal of this story. The accusations of abuse rang so true, I rarely thought to question them. I can't help feeling it was my breach of trust that prompted him to alter his story and leave the program.

"You can still change your mind," I say. "Just stay until you finish high school."

Rodrigo smiles and shakes his head. "This is home," he says.

I know he feels I've betrayed him—like his family, like the system—even if he won't admit it.

"Or at least a trial discharge," I say. "You'll be at home but with the support of the program. You can sign out as soon as you graduate."

Rodrigo looks at the fight that's broken out between one of the boys and the doused girl. She takes off her earrings and throws them at his feet. People start to gather. The girl swings wildly at the boy. The crowd grows.

"They my family. I belong here," he says as the boy pushes the girl, and she falls, blocked from view by the spectators.

Rodrigo shakes my hand, then gathers his backpack and sketch pad. "I'll come by the house sometime."

We both know that's not going to happen.

"Finish school, Rodrigo."

He nods and gets out of the van. "Wish me luck," he says, then walks away.

He passes through the courtyard, past the fight that has all but ended, past the boys on their benches. One of them calls out, *"Puto sucio!"* and they all laugh. Rodrigo smiles at them weakly, tucks his sketch pad under his arm, and opens the battered metal door to the building. He looks back before entering and gives me that big-cheeked grin of his when he sees I'm still there.

CHAPTER 4

THE COLOR OF LEAVES

On the Fourth of July, when I was five years old, my younger brother Lavan and I were left alone at my mother's apartment. Everyone in the building was getting ready to celebrate the holiday. My mother had gone out. My father no longer lived with us. A lot of men came through our apartment, but that day a young black man named David was there. My father was with a Caucasian woman he cheated on my mother with.

David stayed with us a short while after my mother left, revealing to us how restless he can be. When he left, he didn't tell us where he was going and never said when he'd return.

Moments later, Lavan discovered a firecracker. But it wasn't any ordinary firecracker. It was an M-80. Being curious children, Lavan and I decided to light the M-80, wondering what would happen.

When the stick ignited, the lace began to spark. We didn't expect the spark and got freaked out. I told Lavan to put it out with water but he couldn't reach the kitchen faucet.

Panicking, I told him to throw it outside. As Lavan brought his left hand back to hurl the stick in the air it exploded. Lavan's fingertips dropped and dangled from what was left of his hand. His white nerve endings were exposed and his blood gushed out of his thin veins.

We ran screaming and crying for help. A neighbor out of nowhere grabbed Lavan and instantly wrapped his hand in paper towels. I kept running. I passed three apartment complexes and stopped at the fourth and knocked on the door. When the door opened I saw David with a shipping box full of marijuana on his lap and rolled-up Zig Zags in his hands. I told David that Lavan was dying. David got up, knocking over the box. We ran back toward where the neighbor had Lavan. He told us he called 911 and the ambulance was on the way.

I remember being questioned when the authorities arrived. Paramedics took my brother, and David, for his irresponsibility and the smell of marijuana on him, was taken into police custody. Not wanting to go down alone, David gave up info on my mother, saying that we belonged to her and he knew nothing about what happened. So I didn't have to go into state custody, a neighbor volunteered to keep me for a few days. No social workers were around yet; they'd be coming the next day.

I didn't see my mother for a long time after that day. My father never knew anything until my brother was taken from the hospital to state custody. David is a mystery to me today. I didn't see my father and brother until nine years afterwards. I now have no contact with any of them, and haven't in about four years.

It's ironic that the Fourth of July is known as Independence Day because it became our personal Independence Day as well. To pay my respects to the events of the Fourth of July, I spend that day relaxed. I indulge in the pleasure of being here because anything could have happened. Since then I've moved from place to place and haven't had successful bonds. In fact, I'm just getting over clinical depression and am now dealing with anger issues. This was the beginning of my legacy and the death of the "fantastic" family.

The room is silent after Alexander finishes reading his story. He slides the paper toward me, staring down at the dining room table, where the residents and I have gathered for our first writing group.

"What about this story works for you?" I ask. I glance around the room, which is decked out in Thanksgiving decorations. Everyone stays silent. "Montana?"

She looks up from her notebook, where she's been drawing hearts and skulls and crossbones.

"It's good, I guess."

"How is it good?"

"Don't know." She begins to draw a large "x" over the hearts. "I like the part when he talks about his brother's hand getting all blown up." Reginald and Benny nod in agreement.

With Gena's approval I asked the residents if they'd like to start writing together. It's the only thing I feel capable of giving them. So much of the residents' experience in foster care involves hearing their lives dictated to them; they are rarely participants in the construction of their own narratives. My hope is that by writing their stories they'll gain a greater sense of agency. The invitation to join was open to all the residents. Alexander and Caridad were eager to start, and after a little urging from them, Montana, Benny, and Reginald joined. A new resident named Amanda, a tall and lanky trans girl now occupying Rodrigo's old bed, followed everyone's lead.

"OK, good. Alexander allowed his readers to be present in that scary moment by making the description vivid. We could see his brother's hand and felt their anxiety as they ran for help."

"I woulda been like, 'Bitch, please, that your own damn fault,'" Reginald says. "Carrying around a motherfucking M-80 all lit up like that, playing like it ain't gonna blow any second. That just plain stupid."

"Remember how young they are," I note. "Alexander did a great job of setting up the situation for us. In the first paragraph we know that he's five and his brother is younger. We also know they're home alone."

Reginald tells me he was left alone plenty of times as a young child. "You see any missing fingers on this nigga?" he says, wiggling his large hand in my direction. Some of the other residents laugh. I glance up at Alexander. He's still avoiding everyone's eyes.

"So what Alexander has done in his story is set up a situation that tells the reader something of consequence might occur. Two young children are home alone with explosives present. Sounds potentially dangerous. He's set the scene for us."

Alexander stares at the table. Montana is now slouched in her chair, her forehead pressed against her notebook. Amanda is applying lipstick; Reginald is humming and doing a twitchy dance in his seat, while Caridad focuses on picking out the crud from her bitten-down fingernails.

"Take out a piece of paper," I say.

I ask them to write about a transformative moment for twenty minutes. I use Alexander's story as an example, how he wrote about the time he was first taken from his home and how that changed the course of his life. I tell them to think of a moment that altered the way they saw themselves. "It can be anything, big or small. Write about what happened and how it made you feel." I'm not sure about the exercise and uncertain if what I'm offering is even interesting to the residents.

They fiddle with their pens, shuffle their papers. Reginald uses a pen cap to scrape out the inside of his ear. A cool draft whispers in from the cracked plaster walls. Outside the living room window, russet and yellow leaves, with their burnt and darkened edges, scatter into autumn flurries. As the residents hunch over their papers, I slowly walk around the table. Alexander, Caridad, Benny, Amanda, and Montana all have their noses close to their notebooks, scribbling, but Reginald is staring out the window, his pen held to his temple with his index finger.

"How's it going?" I whisper, and catch a glimpse of his notebook, a spidery jumble of incoherence. From what I can tell, Reginald, who is seventeen, writes with the proficiency of a second grader. I squat down next to him. "Can you think of a moment when something in your life changed?"

"Of course."

"Can you write it down? Just a few sentences. Don't worry about spelling or grammar. It doesn't have to be perfect."

His eyes look tense and his mouth tightens as he peeks at the other residents silently writing. Reginald scoots his chair back. "This shit is mad boring," he says, loudly.

Benny looks up, lets out a heated breath, and slams his pen onto the paper. "Can't you shut up for twenty minutes?"

"Miss thing, go pour yourself a tall glass of fuck off."

Benny's eyes widen. I try to redirect their attention but it's too late. Reginald is amped. He shoots up out of his chair, as if jolted by an electric shock. Benny scoffs, shaking his head. Reginald twirls his index finger upward, syncopated with his swiveling head.

"Bitch, don't play me."

My stomach tightens. It's only a few minutes into our first session and already I'm losing control. Benny starts laughing, which prompts Reginald to kick back his chair, sending it crashing to the floor. All the residents begin whooping and hollering. I wipe away the sweat forming on my forehead.

"Reginald," I say. "Stop."

"You going to try to play me? I'll fuck you up. I'm not pussy, bitch. Try me."

"Reginald!"

Benny looks around the table. "These new bitches coming into this house don't know I come from the last pancake batch of shady girls and will quickly deliver a lesson to the fool who is not aware!" Montana leans in, grinning and giddy, bumps knuckles with Benny.

I ask them to relax and sit down, which they ignore.

"You jealous 'cause nobody wants that ugly ass," Reginald continues.

"I got me a man," Benny says, rising from his seat.

"Let's not—"

"That fat dude? Nigga, please. He don't want you. You taking his money like a bitch and he be tripping on faggots at BBQ's right in front of you. He your man 'cause he bought you a fucking sack of wings and a fucking rib sack? Get the fuck out of here. He don't want you, Miss Honey. Nobody want you. You a fucking hot mess, child."

As retaliatory insults fly from Benny's mouth like shrapnel, I wedge myself between the two of them and try to gently walk Reginald away from the altercation. "How about we move over here?" I say to him, nodding toward the living room.

"Bitch!" he spits out over my shoulder.

"Suck my dick!"

The boys glare at each other until a truce seems to be agreed upon in their silence.

I turn to the other residents. It feels like an electrical current runs through the room. Why did I think I was capable of pulling this off? "Everybody take a breath, let this go, and begin to write. Let's focus on the assignment."

Benny's face crumples as he sits back down. They all clutch their pens and start writing. In the living room, Reginald grabs the remote and switches on the TV.

"I'm sorry," he says to me as I sit next to him, "but them shots needed to be fired. He a fucking jealous bitch."

I should have known that even something as basic as a writing exercise could frustrate Reginald to the point of blowing up. When he comes home from school his book bag is always empty. He claims to have finished his homework in class but doesn't do it there either. I know this because his English teacher calls the group home occasionally, giving me updates. She sees Reginald as independent and resilient in a way that is rare among high school students, but she tells me he refuses to listen or do his work. He plays games and has conversations at full volume during her lectures, and is dismissive when she tries to quiet him. When he's asked to participate he mocks her and refuses to even open up a book. She tells me his behavior isn't limited to her class.

Her class doesn't have enough books for all the students, she says, and the ones she does have are outdated, missing pages. The room is filled past capacity. Some students don't even have proper desks. It's hard enough to compete with the general chatter and unruliness. Reginald's constant show is just too much.

In my nearly eight months on the job she's the only teacher to call the group home, the first to voice concern. When I mention this to her she suggests that other teachers have resigned to the fact that Reginald and other kids living in group homes are lost in the system and would require too much special attention. They're seen as hopeless.

Ms. Celeste told me that at previous schools, as well as his current one, Reginald has been tormented daily for being gay. Although he has the body of a man there's an unmistakable femininity to him. He's a towering presence—standing over six feet tall, with broad shoulders and solid, unsculpted brawn—but his dark and muscled physique is married to a loose swish. In photographs he likes to curl his lip, making him look intimidating. But on the street, as he saunters down the block, the rhythmic click of his hips seems to be more threatening to the neighborhood boys than any snarl.

In school, Reginald has been followed between classes, mocked and threatened for his effeminate walk. Boys grab themselves, tell him to suck their dicks like a good faggot; others glare silently if he happens to make eye contact, hissing that they're going to fuck him up. By the time he was in middle school rumors circulated that he had AIDS. On countless occasions classmates told him he was a disgrace to their race and should kill himself. What school administrators have dismissed as horseplay is nothing short of abuse. He never complained to his mother about the cruelty he experienced at school, fearing she'd blame him, or smack him, for being effeminate. She'd tell him he'd brought it upon himself. Reginald has learned to defend himself vigorously in the hallways and classrooms, never cowering to the herd mentality of his classmates. Whatever he lacks in traditional masculinity, he makes up for in physical strength. If someone swings at him, he swings back twice as hard. Only then, when the ridicule and bullying turns physical, do teachers or the administration intervene.

For Reginald school has never been about learning. It's about finding ways to survive. He's expected to enter into an environment five days a week where his safety is never assured. The act he's built up is a source of protection, a way to use his femininity to entertain, and a way to distance himself from the misery associated with going to school. If the focus can be turned toward his humor, style, or flashes of anger, if he can amuse his way through the day, then perhaps his tormentors will leave him alone for a while. He's never been in a place where learning was an option. Now, when a teacher has shown interest in him, he seems to feel it's too late to care.

With the other residents, we set specific goals, such as high school graduation or finishing their GED. Neither seems possible for Reginald. I'm afraid the extreme alienation and torment he's come up against is going to leave him ill equipped to find a legitimate way to survive once he leaves foster care. I've talked to him about the importance of education, but he's already made up his mind. He's going to do hair for the neighborhood ladies back in the Bronx. He doesn't need a high school diploma for that. Going to class is just procedural, a way to keep the staff at the 401 off his back. In addition, he's expecting to receive his settlement from a car accident a few years ago. He says he'll live off that.

Reginald clicks through the TV stations with the remote. I sit on the edge of the couch and try to make eye contact.

"Expressing yourself in a writing exercise can be frustrating. And telling our own stories can make us feel vulnerable. Would you like me to help you?"

Reginald rolls his eyes and then refocuses them on the TV screen. "I don't need no help with nothing."

When I arrive for my shift the following week, Alexander comes into the office and says he wants to talk. There's typically a fair level of quip to his banter. He's taken to calling me Snowflake, a distinction bestowed on me for being the whitest person he knows. When Amanda first arrived at the 401, Alexander asked me if I knew why she was named Amanda. His answer: "Because she's a man. Duh." Humor in the house is often used to cope with pain. But today there are no jokes at anyone else's expense, and all nicknames have been shelved.

"Ryan, I'm nervous."

Unlike the other residents, who are native to New York, Alexander grew up in suburban Pennsylvania and migrated to New York on his own at age sixteen. There he was known as Sean. Name changes are not uncommon in our program, but most of them come from transgender youth seeking out a name to better align with their gender expression. In Alexander's case, he carried his father's name, and after his family life deteriorated he wanted to erase the rejection and abuse he associated with the name. He chose Alexander because he had read somewhere that it means "one who assists or protects." He mentioned to staff he wanted to become a social worker when he was older.

After being removed from his mother's apartment he was placed first with his grandparents and then in foster care, his burgeoning sexuality causing a greater rift with his relatives. When he turned to his social worker for support, she also told him it'd be best if he changed his mind about being gay. He stayed for a short while with his boyfriend, a young man he met online. Their relationship was volatile from the start, and soon became violent. The boyfriend would fly into a rage at the smallest transgression and come at Alexander with swinging fists. Without a place that felt safe, Alexander became homeless, sleeping in a portable toilet in a nearby park because the door locked. There, crammed onto a plastic stall, with fetid water at his feet, he began to plot his escape to New York. He wanted to come to the city because he thought it'd be easier to fit in. When Alexander met a counselor at a homeless youth shelter who offered him enough money for a one-way bus ticket, he didn't hesitate. The next day, without warning, he left.

Although he was awestruck by the energy of the city, New York wasn't as welcoming as he'd expected. He had trouble finding a place to live and ended up at a church-funded shelter that specialized in youth services. It didn't take long for Alexander to realize he needed to hide his sexuality if he was to survive there. Staff were dismissive of the openly gay and transgender boarders. When Alexander heard that one of his LGBTQ peers had been raped in the shelter and nothing was done about it, he decided to once again risk homelessness. He found himself in the New York foster care system and placed at the 401 a few months after I started working there.

Alexander's suburban upbringing is a source of alienation for him in the house. Benny calls him Oreo—black on the outside, white on the inside—when Alexander listens to his Annie Lennox CDs. Montana mocks him for his measured, nasal tone. But he didn't come to the office to discuss problems with other residents. That's not what weighs so heavily on him today.

Alexander leans forward; his legs bounce. He tells me about his ex-boyfriend, the one he lived with in Pennsylvania. He's tracked Alexander down. He's in New York and has begun to harass Alexander online. He struggles to meet my eye. He twists the hair next to his temple and looks down. "He knows I live here. He's pissed about the way I disappeared. I'm scared what he might do."

I call Gena and ask to how to proceed. She has me write an incident report and call the Anti-Violence Project, having Alexander report the specifics of their interaction. The counselor at AVP suggests he print up the email exchanges, photocopy them, and send them to their office to see if there is a blatant threat to his well-being and if the police should be notified. When we hang up the phone I look at Alexander.

"Can we make an agreement?" I ask. "Enough with these guys who don't respect you. You're a bright, handsome, and kind young man. It's time to start surrounding yourself with people who can see that in you." Alexander tries to smile; I try to reassure him of his safety. The agency will work with AVP and the police if necessary to protect him from any potential harm. His leg bounces as he twists his hair. He stares out and chews the inside of his lip.

A few days earlier, Alexander had come into the office and handed me folded sheets of notebook paper. He said writing the story for our group had got him thinking, and he'd contacted his mother by phone for the first time in years. When she recognized his voice he heard her disappointment. She didn't ask where he was living, didn't ask if he was OK. Alexander said the conversation was forced and ended abruptly after only a few minutes. I asked him to sit next to me. He was breathing fast; I moved my hand across his back to calm him.

"I started to write my story. My whole story," he told me. "I'm calling it 'The Color of Leaves.' I want you to read what I have so far." He nodded to the folded notebook pages in my hand.

I've heard Alexander's stories. How his father abandoned him, how his mother disappeared, leaving a child to fend for himself. Then how his grandparents forced him to watch straight porn when they suspected he was gay, and brought over young women with the hopes of "curing" him. Although he had the courage to leave, he never gave up hope that his family would accept him. Even after they berated him for being a faggot, even after they denounced his birth in moments of anger, told him never to come back, he waited for acceptance. He continues to wait.

"Alexander, I'll be glad to read it."

As he left the room I unfolded the pages.

"Mama," it began, "When I look for you all I can see is your back."

The following week, only Reginald shows up for our second, and final (I'd come to find out), writing group. Gena warned me this might happen and not to take it personally. Follow-through without an obvious incentive can be difficult to maintain for the residents. We wait a half hour, looking out the window at the gray, sleeting sky. I ask him if he's interested in having a writing session—just the two of us—and he hesitates. "Do I got to write?" he asks.

"How about we skip that part for now." I settle in a chair at the dining room table. Reginald sits across from me. "We can find a topic, describe it, and discuss how it makes you feel."

I ask Reginald what topic he'd be interested in discussing. He stares back blankly. I suggest a story about his aspirations, or maybe he could describe something he saw today on the way to school. He looks down and says, "What you had us do last week?"

I remind him that the assignment was to describe a transformative moment in his life. He nods. "That one. I'ma tell you about that." Slowly his attention focuses on his story. He begins to tell me about his turning point, the instant he realized everything would be different. He starts slow, but as he falls into the world of the story the words build momentum, lift with life, until they fire out of him.

He was twelve when it first happened. Reginald remembers hammering at the handset of the video game he was playing while waiting for his uncle to return from the bathroom. Around him on the couch were magazines of naked girls. On the coffee table where he propped up his feet was a plastic cup of fruit punch and a bottle of vodka. Near the VCR, a pile of videos. Down the hall a distant smoke detector in need of new batteries faintly chirped. Reginald liked this apartment. The entryway of his housing project smelled like pee; this place was sweet and fragrant. The windows from the room he shared with his mother were clouded with soot, cracked, and the kitchen and bathroom floors had missing tiles. The windows here were clear, looking out into a courtyard with a flower garden. The kitchen floor shined. At home there were no video games, and none of this attention.

When his uncle came back from the bathroom he suggested they turn off the game. Reginald noticed his uncle's fly was unzipped but didn't say anything. There was something he wanted to show Reginald, something cool.

"Take a drink of this," he said, handing Reginald the cup. When Reginald swallowed the red liquid a metallic heat trailed down his throat and burned his stomach.

Reginald's uncle had recently re-entered his life after a long absence and started showing up at the recreation center where Reginald goes after school. Out of nowhere his uncle started showing interest in him, calling him special, while others ridiculed or ignored him. He commented on how Reginald had grown up so fast, and asked what he liked to do for fun. He told him about how great his apartment was, how he had a PlayStation but no one to play it with. One *day he suggested they skip the recreation center and go to his house. Reginald agreed.*

Inside the apartment, his uncle commented how hot it was, told Reginald to take off his shirt. He put a video into the VCR and Reginald did as he was told. On the screen flashed images of a naked man and a naked woman, their bodies entwined. Reginald could feel his uncle standing over him looking down. A pulse began to rise at his center. He placed his hands over his lap, embarrassed. His uncle reached down with his meaty hands, tugged at Reginald's shorts, releasing him from his underwear. Reginald stayed as still as he could, his eyes focused on the screen, his heart beating through his chest.

"It's OK," his uncle said. "You gotta practice so you know what to do when you got a girl."

He leaned down, forcing Reginald's legs open. Closing his eyes tight, Reginald felt warmth around him, then a pressure he couldn't control building at his center. He told his uncle to stop, that he had to pee, but that only made his uncle go faster.

Everyone had always mocked Reginald, tried to beat the differences out of him, but his uncle seemed to like what he saw. All his life Reginald had wanted to know he mattered to someone. But he wasn't the way boys are supposed to be. That difference, he knew, made him unlovable. Now here was his uncle, telling him he's wonderful, giving him the attention he'd always craved. Now he knew of a place to go when his loneliness ate at him. When ridiculed by his father, who called from prison, beaten by his mother, or bullied at school, he knew this man could help relieve that pain. Reginald pushed down the shame growing inside when he thought about what others would say if they knew what he was doing. He couldn't allow that to get in the way of what he needed. His uncle told him he was special and that's all that mattered. As Reginald tolerated his uncle's pawing hands, he focused on the sound of the fire alarm down the hall, its frantic, muffled distress call, too faint for anyone else to hear.

The next day, Laura and I are sitting in the office at the 401. She's huddled in her winter coat, blowing on her pale hands and rubbing them together. Even with the heat cranked the house never gets warm. Laura is waiting for Alexander to show up for their therapy appointment, and as we sit in silence she picks up a magazine, wets her finger, and turns the page. I watch her eyes pass over the words and build up the courage to mention my concern for Reginald. After he disclosed being molested to me I reported it to the administrative staff and documented the whole exchange. Laura talked privately with Reginald this morning.

She closes her magazine and tucks one leg underneath her. She tells me Reginald seems detached from the emotional reality of his story. "He appears to see his abuse as normal. As if it's the only form of attention he deserves." When I ask what I can do to help, she suggests we help him work toward improving his sense of self-worth.

I tell Laura about the first time I met Reginald, when I drove him to the ninety-nine-cent store for some supplies he needed for his room. At a stoplight he leaned close to me. "You like young black boys?" he asked, reaching over, touching my thigh. "I be whatever you want." My cheeks flushed with color. I told him that kind of talk was inappropriate, that I was staff and he was a resident. While staring forward, I asked him to remove his hand. The cross traffic finally yielded to the stoplight and our van lurched forward into the intersection. Reginald hesitated, then lifted his hand from my lap and looked out the window.

"So many of our residents are confused by kindness," Laura says, brushing a blond curl from her forehead. "They sexualize relationships because they've never seen what a healthy relationship with an adult looks like. Relating to another person can be complex because it forces us to relate to a part of ourselves."

I hear the front door open, and with it, Alexander's voice. He's talking about how damn cold it is in this house. Laura gets up and collects her belongings, makes her way to the door to begin their session. "Reginald's response isn't uncommon, unfortunately," she says. "He's seeking out the only kind of affection he feels worthy of."

The next week Gena is sitting in the office with Ms. Celeste. Both look somber when I enter the room. I ask where everyone is, and I'm told the residents were sent to school early. Gena asks me to close the door. I do as I'm told and sit down. She tucks a strand of hair behind her ear. When she tells me Reginald is upstairs, I sense something is wrong. I'm told he came forward the previous night, shaken, and told Ms. Celeste that he needed to go to the doctor. After she pressed him to disclose the problem, he confessed he'd been raped.

"Oh," is all I manage to say, feeling sick from the news. I'm frozen, staring back in silence. Ms. Celeste tells me Reginald admitted to her that it was a man he was dating. Reginald went to his place to do his hair. Things became physical. This time, the man wanted to push things further than usual. Reginald protested; the man insisted. Now that the truth has come out, he's refusing to go to the hospital or talk to the police. He's afraid something will happen to the man. Laura tried to talk with him this morning, but he wouldn't have it.

"Reginald doesn't want to press charges and because he's reached the age of consent, there's nothing we can do." Gena asks me to talk to Reginald, see if I can persuade him to go to the police. I want to flee. Instead I walk upstairs.

Reginald's room is dark and cold. He's in bed, buried under a heap of covers. I sit near his feet, pat his leg, and say hi. He moves away.

We sit in silence for a while until I ask, "Do you feel comfortable talking about what happened last night?"

Reginald looks up from his covers and, to my surprise, nods.

I start by saying he did nothing wrong and he rolls his eyes.

"Oh, my God, I know. Why everybody keep saying that? The problem is the pain."

I realize he's probably never had the sex talk. Queer kids don't normally have that kind of guidance. If schools offer sexual education, it's typically the standard "birds and bees" speech, the obligatory lecture about how a man and a woman come together to make a baby. In most cases, the only mention of homosexuality is during AIDS discussions. And transgender people never find themselves represented in these conversations. LGBTQ youth have to figure out things for themselves. Through trial and error, mostly error, they come to an understanding of how to traverse a confusing sexual landscape.

Reginald tells me he doesn't want to go to the doctor anymore. He's afraid his business will be "put on blast" and he doesn't want anything to happen to his abuser. I choose to focus on the immediate health concerns, hoping if I can get Reginald to see a doctor, the story will naturally unfold. I'm unsure how exactly to proceed, though, and my intention to gently finesse the facts out is hindered by nerves.

"Something could have torn if he didn't use lubrication," I blurt out.

"He used lube," Reginald says.

"Was he safe?"

Reginald doesn't answer. He glances at me like he wants to say something. "It hurts on the outside," he says, looking at the door, then to me. "Maybe I got ripped?"

I'm not sure how to answer. "Was he aggressive with you?"

Reginald nods. "Kinda. And he mad big," he says and holds his hands out as if measuring a hero sandwich. I look away, hope the red I feel flooding my cheeks isn't too obvious.

"If he's large it'd be harder for your body to adapt."

I don't know if what I'm saying is entirely true, but I hope that if there's enough authority in my voice, it'll miraculously become accurate.

Reginald glances back at the open door. I reassure him the house is empty; all the residents are at school or work.

"Will you look?" he asks me. "Tell me if I torn it."

"I'm not the person to do that. We can get you to a doctor, though."

He shakes his head and closes his eyes. Something swells inside me, and I reach forward and touch Reginald's cheek. He looks at me, startled.

"Listen," I say, my voice shaky. "You need to let us take care of you now. I know it's scary, but you need to see a doctor to make sure you're healthy."

The pleading in my voice surprises us both. Reginald searches my face.

"Please," I say, struggling through the rise of tears. "Let us help you."

Reginald took some convincing to get him to agree to a hospital visit. We went back and forth about the possible health risks involved with unprotected sex. He swore he was fine, that he only thought something had torn. I told him he needed to see a doctor precisely because the sex was unprotected.

The hospital waiting room is white-tiled and lined with cheap folding chairs filled with grumpy, sick people. There are more individuals than spaces to sit, so a few patients are lined up against the wicker baskets filled with fake, plastic plants. I think about offering up my seat, but don't.

Reginald walks out from behind a white door and gestures for me to come up to meet him at the triage station. From what he's been prescribed—an ointment, some painkillers—I assume he wasn't entirely honest with the doctor about what happened. And although I know I should speak up, something anchors my voice. I show his Medicaid number for the third time, sign a form, take the yellow copy, and walk toward the exit.

"I was right," Reginald says, as the glass doors open automatically and the cold whips in. He has a wide, sunny grin, beaming about what he must see as a rite of passage. "He ripped my asshole," Reginald says.

Thanksgiving arrives quickly. The city feels heavy and gray, wrapped in a perpetual chill. I sit alone in the living room at the 401, then get up to peer out the window, stare at the bare, wet street. Benny is at his stepfather's, Caridad is in Harlem with her family, Amanda has been given a pass to stay with a friend. Reginald is in the Bronx with his mother. Alexander has calmed down about his ex-boyfriend now that the boy has returned to Pennsylvania. For weeks, he had been afraid to leave the house, sure that he was being watched. Tonight he has ventured out to share Thanksgiving with Montana and her mother. For the first time, there are no residents to look after. An eerie, empty quiet fills the house.

I'm surprised when Ms. Celeste stops by to bring me a plate piled with turkey, collard greens, homemade macaroni and cheese, and sweet potato pie, even though I didn't ask for anything. She stays long enough for me to sample her macaroni and cheese. When she returns to her family, I sit and eat her food alone, watching *Roseanne* reruns. Because the cold in the house is unbearable, I turn on the oven and leave the door open.

I walk into the office. Reginald's sweatshirt is draped over the back of Gena's chair. Just hours before, he was at the office computer looking for friends and family members on the Department of Corrections website, as if it were meant for social networking. Every resident in the group home has been affected by incarceration, watching as cops have roughed up their fathers, uncles, cousins, locking them up for crimes both real and imagined. Reginald refused to talk to the cops about his rape when another counselor took him to the police station. His distrust makes sense. I've witnessed how police officers tense up when Reginald walks into a store, not realizing I'm accompanying him. He has only seen law enforcement belittle and humiliate people in his community. Trust is difficult to cultivate with the residents. They've all been let down so many times before, failed by those who were tasked with protecting them.

Autumn begins to creep into winter. At a time when I'm getting close to most of the residents, I've decided it's time for me to leave. I've applied for Steve's caseworker position at Keap Street now that he's moving into the role of house manager, managing the residential counselors and overseeing group home operations. The job frightens me. Keap Street is a twelve-bed house, double the size of the 401. Twice as big means twice as many problems. With that will come more responsibility, more pressure to perform. Whereas with the residential counselor position I work with the youth on day-to-day skills, a caseworker focuses more on big-picture issues, meeting program goals. Caseworkers meet with family members to work toward reunification or independent living; they represent the agency in Family Court during permanency planning hearings and scrupulously document all interactions with the youth and their family. It's a whole new set of responsibilities I'm unsure I know how to meet.

To my surprise, Jessica offers me the position. I tell myself this opportunity is about change, and change is about moving forward. I want to be more a part of the mission of the program, to be of greater service to the youth. Despite my uncertainties and the stories about how out of control the residents are at Keap Street, I take the job.

Laura suggested I tell everyone at the 401 I'm leaving a month before my departure. She said transitions are hard for so many of the youth. They've been abandoned so many times. It's important they understand my leaving isn't about desertion.

As a way to celebrate my new position and commemorate my time at the 401, Alexander and Reginald decide to make me dinner. They've prepared steak and vegetables they found in the freezer. When we sit at the dining room table, I'm so touched by the gesture I barely notice that the meat is cooked to resemble tree bark and the broccoli is slippery and limp. I happily shovel the food in my mouth.

"You seen *Boondocks* today?" Reginald asks Alexander.

As a way to get him more comfortable with reading, I started discussing the comic strip with Reginald every morning.

"That shit was off the hook."

We talk about Huey Freeman's criticism of the Bush administration in the comic strip, then the conversation moves on to school and their goals for the future. I look at Alexander and Reginald, and realize how well I've come to know and respect them.

Alexander peers out the window as we finish our meal. Snow flurries are beginning to fall around the house. "Look," he says, glancing back to me. "Your relatives have come to visit." My laugh is quiet at first, then gradually becomes louder, until I hide my wet eyes.

As we begin clearing the dishes from the table Caridad walks in and picks a hunk of broccoli from my plate, inspects it, and tosses it back. "Keap Street is mad crazy," she says to me. "You even know where you're going?" I balance the stack of dishes in my hand, walk into the kitchen, careful not to lose poise, knowing with one uncertain shift, everything could come crashing down.

"No," I say, and look back to her. "No, I don't."

KEAP STREET

CHAPTER 5

NO AFTER-SCHOOL SPECIAL

The apartment is in East New York, Brooklyn, on a street scarred with empty storefronts. The building's buzzer is broken, so I call from a pay phone at the corner bodega to let him know I'm here. When the door opens, a thick man with charcoal skin looks down at me. His dark eyes first take me in, then scan the street, the sidewalk. "You the caseworker?" he asks.

"Yes," I say, but before I can extend my hand he turns around and walks up the stairs.

"Shut the door behind you."

I'm two months into my new role as the caseworker for Keap Street, and this is my first time meeting Barbara's father for a mandatory home visit. Each month I'm required to have face-to-face contact with the parents of the youth at their homes as a way to stay in touch, in an attempt to make them a part of their children's lives while at the same time assessing the home environment to make

sure it's safe for the child to return. I was warned about
him. Jessica told me about his blatant homophobia and
dislike for our program. Reunification with the family is
a top priority of the agency, but in this case—as in most
cases with the population we serve—it is very unlikely.
Barbara's father is completely hostile toward her, Jessica
said. He refuses to take any responsibility for the state of
their relationship. I've been warned that his behavior is
unpredictable, even explosive. The last caseworker, Steve,
was ushered out after only a few minutes. He challenged
Barbara's father on his homophobia and unwillingness to
accept his daughter for who she is. Steve reported that the
father was volatile and potentially violent.

At the office, I had gathered my things into my
backpack and slid the piece of paper with directions to
his apartment into my pocket. Heavy caseloads and budget cuts meant caseworkers were unable to operate in
pairs—a safety precaution—as was strongly suggested
during training. As I made my way out of the building
that evening, Gladyce grabbed me by my jacket sleeve.
"Don't let him know you're gay," she said, raising a pen-
ciled eyebrow and holding my gaze before taking another
long drag of her Virginia Slim.

The apartment is cluttered with piles of magazines,
photo albums, and heaps of unopened mail. I notice the
agency's logo on an envelope peeking out of a mound of
papers on the coffee table. When I look closer I recognize

my own handwriting and realize that it's a letter I sent about a month ago, requesting this visit. The envelope appears to be unopened. I'd succeeded in setting up this meeting only after I made a series of phone calls to a number Barbara gave me. Nobody answered the home phone listed in the case file, but this number was her father's cell, she told me. My first attempts went to his voicemail: "Yo, this is Darkstar," a muscular voice announced. "If you need to get at me, you know what to do." Finally, after several tries, he answered, and only after I stressed that home visits were mandatory did I get him to agree to my coming to see him.

"Punch?" A woman with brittle, orange hair hands me a beverage. I take it, thank her, and without removing my jacket, sit down, balancing the drink on my knee.

"Babe, you want some?" she asks, walking back into the narrow kitchen behind me. "Babe? You want some Hawaiian Punch?"

"You know it," he says, brushing a stack of papers off the couch, settling low across from me, his legs separating in a wide V shape with his heavy hands resting on his thighs. The thermal work suit he's wearing is unzipped, revealing a postal service uniform underneath. "My wife," he says, looking at me, not at her. "Barbara didn't treat her with no respect." I'd spent most of the morning reviewing Barbara's case file so I could better understand the family dynamic. I knew that she had little contact with her mother, who was a crack addict at the time of Barbara's birth. After a series of foster care placements as a baby, she was eventually put in the custody of her paternal grandmother at the age of six and lived with her and her aunt until the grandmother died a few years ago. The aunt was unable to continue caring for Barbara because of her own declining health. That's when she moved in with her father and stepmother, and the trouble began.

"Trouble. That's what she is, don't be fooled," Barbara's stepmother calls out from the kitchen.

"She got everybody fooled with that smile," he says, nodding.

"Nobody going to disrespect me in my own home." She walks back into the living room and places her husband's drink on one of the thick piles of paper in front of him. "In my own home," she says again, resting her hand against her hip. "That's some nerve."

Outside, bare tree branches scrape up against the apartment windows as light snow scatters into winter flurries. Across the street, Christmas lights still blink almost two months after the fact. I pretend to sip the dayglo fuchsia in my cup and scan the apartment: bare windows with one cracked pane, exposed brick, a fireplace containing a stack of magazines, a beaten-down piano, an antique standing lamp in the corner, mismatched furniture, a sewing machine, an iron on top of the TV. I'm unsure what I'm looking for. If there are telltale signs of an unsafe home, they were never divulged during my four weeks of training.

Barbara's stepmother goes back into the kitchen and begins to prepare dinner. The honeyed smells of browning meat fill the room along with the crackle and squeak of grease bubbling in the pan. It seems that the necessities are accounted for here: food, shelter. Clutter, I'm sure, isn't a crime. To my left a door is slightly ajar, a thin thread of light escapes out onto the living room floor.

"That's her room," Barbara's father says. He's been watching me search his apartment.

"*Was* her room," the stepmother says from the kitchen, "for two years." I place the plastic cup down on the table between us.

"When was the last time you spoke with your daughter?"

"When the courts put her into that lesbian place she's at now. No daughter of mine is going to walk around thinking she's a boy." We look at each other blankly for a moment.

"Mr. Richards, Barbara doesn't identify as a boy," I say. "Regardless of how she sees herself, I think she's more concerned about having the support a sixteen-year-old needs. Adolescence can be a difficult time."

He leans forward. "This ain't no after-school special, son. You a girl, you dress like one. You a boy, you do the same. That's the way it is. Anything else is unnatural.

You hear what I'm saying, right?" He stares at me. "That last caseworker, damn, that faggot didn't get it." My eyes drop to the floor as I shift in my seat, folding my hands then quickly unfolding them, finally placing them on my knees.

"I'm not sure it's that cut and dry," I reply, my voice growing deeper, more measured than normal. Barbara's father then leans back with a sigh and spreads his legs. Looking at me, he rolls his tongue beneath his lower lip then sucks his teeth. His hand drops to his crotch, gripping the fabric, the bulk of his groin plump in his hand. He casually rubs himself through his work suit.

"There's some devious shit out there," he says, staring at me.

A rush of heat fills my face. I can't quite meet his gaze but refuse to allow my eyes to fall and focus on the movement below. His wife continues to assemble their dinner just behind me. The sounds of her movements, harried. There's the scrape of potatoes being whipped, then the direct clout of the spatula on the rim of the bowl. I hold my breath for fear of what she might witness.

My upper lip begins to tremor. The ripple seems to run the course of my body into my bent legs and through the taut tendons of my feet pressing the floor. A cool sweat collects at the nape of my neck. I can feel his eyes on me as I lean down to my bag and begin to sift through papers. My breathing escalates, my pulse quickens. I can't look up at him until I'm calm, I tell myself. I can't let him see me flustered.

"I'm sure there is," I say, my throat tight, "but that has nothing to do with Barbara." He scoffs and scratches his groin one last time before stretching his arm along the back of the couch.

"You hear that, babe? Nothing to do with Barbara."

He presses himself even further back on the couch now with both arms stretched out; his legs flap open and closed. I'm sure I'm being tested. If my eyes had dropped to his fondling hand, would that have made me the thing he must assume I am? Less than a person, asking for it. I think about my co-worker's warning before I left the office and wonder if Barbara's father is trying to entrap me, to fool me, to give him reason to kick another case-worker out of his apartment.

The clatter of frying pans in the kitchen pulls me back to the living room. Looking up in the direction of Barbara's father, I return to work.

"She's shown considerable improvement since being placed with us. Her teachers all say she's really bright and has made a lot progress considering the length of time she's been out of school. I have a letter from her math teacher if you want to read it."

He says nothing, only pokes the tip of his tongue out, licking the corner of his mouth as if trying to locate some rogue crumb.

"You don't know that girl, the crazy shit she be doing," he says.

I look up at the wall clock, which has paused at 3:45. The entire scenario begins to feel absurd, and I can't help but wonder if my mind invented the whole thing. Maybe he only scratched an itch and I somehow drew time out into a slow-motion event, seeking an undercurrent of meaning that wasn't there. Maybe my discomfort fashioned him into a menacing caricature. I'm suddenly ashamed by the starkness of my own prejudice.

"Well, she's doing really well in our program," I say, my voice shaking. "We're hoping to find her a part-time job too." The corners of his mouth lift causing his cheeks to dimple.

"Y'all right in the palm of her hand," he says. "She got y'all fooled."

Barbara's stepmother walks into the living room, her hand inside an oven mitt pressed against her hip. "She'll fuck up—excuse the language—but she will. You just watch."

I tell her that I know there has been trouble with Barbara, that their home life was a challenge with her here, but didn't she think there was room for reconciliation? She removes her oven mitt, holds it under her armpit, then dusts her hands off, showing me her palms. "I wash my hands of that child."

When I look back at Barbara's father he's staring off, distant from our conversation. He no longer seems the same man from moments before. His features are softer, less aggravated. He sighs and turns his head away from his wife. Something about that brief moment of vulnerability draws me to him. I see in that instant that he feels something for his daughter that he doesn't dare show. As his shoulders drop and his chest collapses with an exhaling breath, Barbara's father no longer seems concerned with asserting his authority. I catch a glimpse of a man hidden beneath the parade of his exteriors.

I know caring for his daughter has been an unexpected burden, financially and emotionally. In training I learned that receiving a low income can be a strong risk factor for all forms of maltreatment. What little money he had was stretched thin when they took Barbara in. The stress from poverty can result in greater risk of depression, anxiety, drug use, and community violence, and tipping-point frustrations can lead to abuse. I can't help but feel Mr. Richards had the odds stacked against him when he accepted to house Barbara. But these facts don't excuse his indifference or his abandonment of his daughter.

I look at him, with his large hands clasped tight at his knees, and wonder what he has left unsaid. The stepmother begins to shift her weight from side to side.

"Taking in a stepchild can be a big undertaking," I say. "There can be a lot of feelings, a lot of changes."

"You got that right," she says. "That little bitch try and tell me my business, like I don't know." My eyes stay fixed on Barbara's father, Darkstar, a man so prone to posturing that, without even a hint of irony, he named himself as if he were a superhero. I imagine he hides behind masks, bravado, constructing his masculinity to shelter himself from anything that could pose a threat to his feeling of control.

"Do you feel the same way, that you've washed your hands of your daughter?" I ask. He sits quietly for a moment. Then he shoots his gaze at me, his features again hardened.

"I don't even know if she's mine," he says. "Her mother's a crack whore, probably sold that ass for a piece of rock a million times." I look at his wife, who's nodding her head, her arms now crossed around her thick middle. I look back at him.

"You don't believe Barbara's your daughter?"

"She looks like her mother, not me."

"You don't believe Barbara's your daughter?" I repeat. He rubs his palms flat on his knees.

"I'm sorry, but even if she isn't biologically yours, you've raised her, your mother raised her. Now you just abandon her?"

Silence fills the room. Only a creak from the floorboards is heard as the stepmother shifts her weight. Barbara's father grips the fabric of his work suit over his knees. I wish I hadn't said what I did. But Barbara's father doesn't rise from the couch with a flare of anger like I imagined.

Instead he tells me how he found out about Barbara when he returned from the Gulf War in 1992. She was young and had been living in a series of foster care placements. When his mother heard that Barbara was his child, she insisted he take responsibility for his actions. He wasn't able to take her in, so his mother and sister did, raised Barbara from that time until his mother passed away two years ago when Barbara was fourteen.

"I was married by the time Barbara came to stay here," he says. "She wouldn't listen. She was in the streets, dressing and acting like a boy. Disrespecting my wife. She never do as she's told."

"Somebody ought to smack some sense into that child," the stepmother says. "I bet you she wouldn't be all gangster if she got knocked on her ass." I ignore her and continue to press him.

"Things aren't good between you and your daughter."

He sits back, his arms crossed around his barrel chest. "She's a crackhead and probably selling her ass now too, how're things supposed to be good?"

I look at him intently. The fear I had felt moments ago evaporates with the hollow clink of his accusations. "We both know she doesn't smoke crack or prostitute," I say. "Mr. Richards, Barbara isn't her mother."

He averts his eyes and becomes restless in his seat. He seems uncomfortable, as if he imagined I might have seen something through the tough veneer that he works so hard to maintain. I imagine Barbara as a child eating dinner with her father, his inability to look at her because she resembled her mother so much. Maybe he couldn't separate the two of them in his mind. Maybe, for him, they fused into one person, and forced him to continually collide with a past that he wanted to forget.

I know from reading the case file that he is opposed to outside involvement. He sneers at the idea of therapy, says he isn't crazy and doesn't need a shrink telling him he is. Before I left to meet him this evening, Jessica told me that I'd have to avoid words that would put up red flags for him. Don't mention therapy; don't use words like "mediation."

"It seems like you and Barbara have a hard time speaking to each other without fighting." He nods, rubs his hand against his cheek.

"Maybe it'd be helpful to have someone there to make it easier for you guys to talk through things. Like a middleman. Someone who can bring things back before they escalate out of control."

"I ain't doing therapy," he says.

"I'm not talking about that. I'm talking about finding a way to communicate again with your daughter."

Barbara's stepmother has made her way back into the kitchen, grumbling something about dinner getting cold and that company should know when to leave. I write my number down on an envelope in case he needs to get in touch with Barbara, wants to take initiative and begin mending their relationship.

"You know, I never said nothing about abandoning her. She's trouble now. That's all I'm saying." I look up from my pen and paper to find him staring down at his hands.

"We used to get along real good. When she was little and living with my mom I'd take her to the zoo and she'd get all excited about the animals, smiling like crazy. I got a picture of that, you want to see?"

"He don't want to see no picture," his wife hollers.

Barbara's father stands up and takes a step in his wife's direction, his arms extended, slapping at the air. "Nobody asked you, woman."

He then walks into the room that was once his daughter's. When he returns he's carrying a large, glossy photograph the size of a magazine cover, hands it to me. In it Barbara's wearing a baby blue sweater with pink streaks. A white belt is peeking out just above the zipper of her acid-wash jeans. Her hair is short and frizzy. I'm not startled by the image of Barbara in girl's clothing, as I imagined I would be. Even then she looked out of place in feminine clothes. Her eyes are fixed on the boa constrictor coiled around both her and her older brother's shoulders. She stares closely at the patterned scales of its skin, her hands pulling close to her chest, not yet ready to touch. She seems unaware of the camera; she doesn't smile, but a slight expression of awe brightens her face.

Her brother cups the snake's head in one hand, looking down, smiling. Barbara's father stands behind his children, the only one looking into the camera, a full white-toothed grin fills his face. He's wearing army fatigues and a camouflage cap. His broad shoulders span the width of both of his children. His hands aren't resting on their shoulders, there's no evidence of contact. He's just there, posing for the camera, as he knows a father should, maybe the way his father did. Looking the role but, I imagine, never really knowing how to fulfill the function.

"It's a nice picture," I say. "You all look happy."

He seems caught up in the memory of the photograph until his wife calls out from the kitchen and that toughness shows up on his face again. I try to hand back the photograph but he walks to the front door, shaking his head.

"No," he says, turning the knob and exposing the hallway. "That's for you, you can keep it."

I'm surprised when Barbara walks into my office, sits down, and acts like nothing's new. She's been AWOL from the group home for a month now. I think she's living with her girlfriend's family but there's no way to be sure. Things were going well until her father and stepmother showed up at court for her permanency planning hearing, where the judge must determine the appropriateness of the agency's long-term plan for the youth and the reasonableness of the agency's efforts to execute the plan. Before entering the courtroom they cornered Barbara, berated her, and disowned her for acting like a boy. If she put on a dress, he'd consider supporting her, her father said, but as she is, she is an abomination. I tried to separate them, to shield Barbara from his words, but by the time we were ushered in to see the judge, she was trembling.

I was there to tell the court that Barbara had improved since coming to the program. She was placed with the agency after her stepmother filed a Person in Need of Supervision (PINS) petition—a request for the court to intervene when a child becomes out of control. Barbara's stepmother said that she was wild and disrespectful. She'd leave the house for days at a time, was truant from school. The stepmother alleged physical threats and drug abuse. Barbara claims her stepmother just wanted her out of their lives. She says her father was given an ultimatum and chose his wife.

When Barbara came into our care in mid-2004, she began attending school regularly for the first time in nearly two years. Her teachers said she was smart and that she participated in class. She hadn't run away from the group home or stayed out past curfew like she did while living with her father. She never tried to hide her marijuana use, and the agency was working with her on issues of chemical dependency.

On the day of the planning hearing, her father got her so worked up outside the courtroom that when the judge addressed her, she snapped at him.

"See how she acts, Your Honor?" her father said.

Crying, she cursed at him, and had to be escorted out.

When we left court that day, her placement with the agency was extended for another six months. Barbara was silent on the train ride home and studied the advertisements for facial citrus peels in order to avoid conversation. Her face didn't betray any emotion. I told her to forget what her father had said. She was making strides and needed to continue in that direction. The subway car rattled and shook, the lights flickered as we screeched to a halt at her station. "Stay strong," I said. "I'm here for you." She smiled dimly and promised she'd continue to try hard, then turned to exit the subway car.

She went AWOL that night from Keap Street and stopped attending school. She calls occasionally to tell me she's OK but never discloses her location. I hadn't seen her since that day in court, nearly a month ago.

Barbara absently punches the keyboard of my computer with one finger. Pinned up on the wall behind her, along with a list of caseworker telephone extensions and GED test locations, is the large photograph of Barbara standing with her father and brother at the zoo. In the picture there's a youthful innocence about her. That joy, that free expression on her face, is missing from the person I know.

Barbara pulls her camouflage Yankees cap down on her face. She looks frail, like she's stopped eating. The sports jersey she's wearing hangs from her slight frame; she swims in her jeans. Her dark skin is ashen and her eyes look heavy and somber. I don't know how long I'll have her here so I pull out my wallet, drop a twenty into her hand, and tell her to use it for food. She thanks me, smiles, then her eyes fall to her sneakers. When I ask how she's doing she becomes motionless, seems to be holding her breath. She has a sweet disposition. Normally she's good-natured but out of nowhere she can erupt, lashing out for the tiniest transgression. That's a side of her we didn't see much. Typically, when still at the group home, she would be found watching B.E.T. with the other residents, her bright smile exposing a line of perfect, white teeth.

When Barbara arrived at Keap Street the staff loved her right away. Gladyce gushed about her acclimating to the home. "She made her bed in the morning and left for school right on time. This child does her chores and don't need to be told twice about curfew. How on earth did we get this one?" Gladyce said, and then let out a sharp laugh. The honeymoon period ended when Barbara flew into a rage at Dia, another resident, whom she accused of stealing her Nike Air Jordans. Gladyce said it was impossible to de-escalate Barbara's behavior, that it took three counselors to defuse the situation. When Gladyce tried to intervene Barbara bristled and told her to go back to her box of cookies in the office and mind her business. She persisted and Barbara grabbed a candy bar off of the counter, dangled it in front of Gladyce like bait, calling her a hippo. She was unfazed by Barbara's outburst; most of the residents were prone to lashing out. Later Barbara went to Gladyce in her office and apologized, said she didn't know what happened, didn't know why she was so angry.

Barbara is "A.G.," or an "aggressive," a label used in the gay urban community for butch lesbians. She binds her breasts, dresses in baggy jeans and sports jerseys; her hair is set in tight cornrows; occasionally a gold-plated grill covers her front teeth. On the street she's always mistaken for a boy. She has a tough, callous veneer when on the street. She hides her hurt, or at least she used to.

"I can't do it no more, yo," she says with an exhale, and begins to tremble. She makes her hands into fists then opens them, the twenty dropping to her feet. "I can't do it." Her eyes roll toward the ceiling and her body tenses. She flinches so fully that I think for a moment she's having a seizure. Then tears begin to fall. "I got nobody," she says. I wish my office had a door to shut to give us some privacy.

"Come back to the house," I say and roll my chair closer to her, leaning in. "We can make it work." Her face becomes taut until she releases into sobs; her shoulders heave. She no longer hears me. She's alone, deep inside someplace within herself.

"Why you leave me?"

"Leave?" I say. "Barbara, I never—"

She lets out a wail that shakes me.

"Grandma," she calls out. Her head bows. She wipes her wet nose with the ball of her hand. "She the only one who really loved me."

I place my hand on her shoulder and feel how her body trembles. I search for some tissue to give her but only find a balled-up Kleenex with chewed gum buried in the center. I don't have any words that seem appropriate. I know there's nothing I can do to protect her; I'm helpless to provide even a glimmer of hope.

"Come back" is all I can say. We both know it's not enough.

I pick the twenty off the floor and push it back into Barbara's hand. Her cheeks are wet, her breathing stutters. I try to strategize the way a caseworker should: Barbara's safety is paramount and she needs immediate housing, but she refuses to return to the group home, saying it's too chaotic, that she can't put up with the other residents' lying and stealing. I could initiate an emergency respite placement at a different group home outside the LGBTQ program, but I know Barbara won't go. She is stubborn, willing to consider only one option. She wants to be transferred to our apartment program, where residents pair up with one roommate. I've told her time and time again that the program is designed for youth who have shown potential for living independently. The rules are clear. All residents considered for the apartment program have to be functioning well in the group home, do their chores regularly, and follow regulations. They must demonstrate good relationships with other residents, attend school on a regular basis, and have a part-time job. Barbara currently fails to meet any of the criteria.

I plead with her again to return to Keap Street. I'll call her school and see if they'll take her back. Between classes and a part-time job she'll rarely have to see the other residents, limiting the chance of any conflict that might arise. She could be eligible for the apartment program within a few months.

"Then who's gonna watch my stuff when I'm gone? The staff?" Her face sours. "The minute I leave the house you know they gonna jack all my shit."

I know she's right. Even though all the residents have their own cabinets with padlocks to store their belongings, the moment one is left unattended it's broken into. The locks are pried open; the wooden slats of the cabinet are split; and the resident's sneakers, shirts, and caps are swiped and sold on the street. Stealing has become an epidemic in the house. Each time a resident begins to accumulate a wardrobe—the necessary accoutrements of adolescence—everything is stolen.

The program is allotted eight hundred dollars annually per resident for clothing. There's no reimbursement for stolen items. When it's gone, it's gone. The residents who steal from the others have made it big business. The main reason Barbara won't return to Keap Street is because of her old roommate, Maite. Maite had devised a scheme that when the residential staff were downstairs preparing for dinner and the other residents were at night school or work, she'd sneak up to the bedrooms, unlocking the doors with a key she'd swiped from a staff member, and sift through everyone's closet, leaving the house with the most expensive items before anyone could suspect her. It wasn't until Maite was found tossing garbage bags stuffed with her roommate's belongings out the third-story window down to her friend on the street that staff had any idea she was a thief. I promise Barbara that I'll withhold Maite's clothing money, and that she'll get a portion of it to make up for some of the stolen items.

"No," Barbara says. "No way I'm going back there."

When I ask if she can stay with her brother she shakes her head. He just turned eighteen and can't take on the responsibility of his younger sister. I don't even suggest her father as an option. After the court date he was impossible to talk with. He continued the name-calling, the blaming. When I tried to follow up after our meeting, I was met with icy derision. Barbara was my problem, I was told. They were done with her.

Even the youth who function well in foster care are likely to fail once they're out on their own. One study suggests nearly half of New York City's homeless have gone through the foster care system at one time or another and 40 percent of homeless youth in New York City identify as gay, lesbian, bisexual, or transgender.[1] After aging out of the system, over half of the youth remain unemployed. Debilitating depression, anxiety, and addiction affects one-third of this population.[2] Unless there's a visiting resource, an adult who can function as a role model, and a stable, caring presence in their lives, there's little hope of a life off the streets or outside the system.

"What about Rochelle?" I ask.

Barbara has been living with her girlfriend's family off and on since leaving Keap Street. Rochelle is two years older than Barbara and seven months pregnant. According to Jessica, the family's house is on the verge of collapse. Rochelle's mother has ten children, all of whom still live with her. She collects Social Security checks and some of her older children are selling drugs. Other than that, there isn't any income for the family. When Barbara's there, she's just another mouth to feed, which causes tension between Rochelle and her brothers. Barbara wants to get a job to help buy groceries, but because she's only sixteen and isn't attending school she doesn't have her working papers. No one will hire her for any legal work. She told me on the phone around the time she went AWOL that all she wanted was to help raise Rochelle's baby with her, to give that baby a happy life.

"Rochelle told me her brothers don't want me there no more," she tells me now. "And fuck her anyway."

I can tell by Barbara's leaden, lifeless eyes that she's had enough. She's tired of searching for places to stay, of fighting with Rochelle and her brothers. I'm afraid she'll have to resort to survival sex or drug-running in order to feed herself. I pull out a piece of paper and tell her to write down every person she knows. Maybe there's a family member who she hasn't thought about in a while, some distant relative. She holds the pen just above the surface of the paper, drawing circles in the air. She does this a while longer before dropping the pen to the desk.

"Ain't nobody," she says and rises up from the seat. I stand with her and lean against the doorway. I'm not ready for her to leave. I know that when she walks out of my office she'll have no place to go.

"I don't think we're done here," I say, but she's had enough and pushes past me, down the corridor, vanishing into the staircase. For the first time since meeting her I fear I'll never see Barbara again.

Streetlight seeps into my apartment window. The lamp on my nightstand shines from underneath, casting steep shadows against my wall. I pull a bottle of Hornitos

Tequila and a pack of Parliament Lights out of a brown paper bag. On my way home from the office I knew I'd want something to burn the day away. I take a shot just as the phone rings. Too drained to talk to anyone, I just sit. After the fourth ring my answering machine clicks on.

"Ryan, it's Gladyce."

I stand up and walk over to the voice.

"Somebody stopped by the house and wanted to talk to you."

"Hi Ryan," the voice is quiet, childlike. "It's Barbara."

I lean down and turn up the volume.

"I just wanted to say thanks for today. And I wanted to tell you I thought of somebody. I got a cousin down South. I want to try and live with her."

When I hear the receiver hang up, I move back to my bed and sit down. The silence of my empty room rings in my ears. I reach for the bottle and think of Barbara's prospects. I take a swig of tequila and it goes down like warm ribbons of amber. Thinking of Barbara's future, I want to feel something like relief, but I can't.

CHAPTER 6

THINGS FAMILIES DO

I pull the bill of my baseball cap down over my eyes to shield them from the glaring camera lights. Out in the darkness I can make out blurred silhouettes of people as they move. Next to me Christina straddles her broken school chair. She flings her hair back and rubs her chin into the smooth brown skin of her shoulder, batting her eyes at the shadowed audience in front of us as if they were paparazzi. This might be the closest she gets to her fifteen minutes of fame, and she's not about to let it go. Raheem, seated on the other side of me, slouches, picks at a hangnail, eyes downcast, avoiding the camera light. I'm stuffed into a small chair made for someone less than half my size, trying to calm myself, but my legs continue to jitter and my eyes fight for focus.

"For those of you watching at home and here in our audience, tonight we're going to end with some special guests," a voice announces, amplified with an electric crackle by the gymnasium loudspeakers. "They're in foster care just like the rest of the kids we've seen tonight, but they're a part of the GLF . . . " I can see the interviewer in the darkness standing next to the cameraman, fumbling through his notes. "The GLT . . . "

I'm afraid he's going to call us a BLT, so I lean forward into the microphone, my voice barely scraping out of me. "LGBTQ," I say.

No one's watching at home. We're on Brooklyn's public access channel.

I'm exhausted from eleven hours of work and little sleep. I was fielding phone calls all day from truancy officers, trying to set up meetings with the law guardians who represent the youth in Family Court, in between writing three UCRs—comprehensive service assessments completed twice a year for each youth—all due tomorrow. Not to mention my futile attempt at trying to register a new resident for school. I trekked all the way over to Keap Street before heading to the agency's Brooklyn headquarters, where my office is located, in order to escort her on her first day. Staff didn't bother to call and let me know she had been out all night. Now I'm here in Harlem at 7:00 p.m. for an adoption open house for teenagers. But even if it's exhaustion that sets off my irritation, now that we're up here I can't help feeling like they've put us on display, saved the freaks for last. I know they want to show they're progressive and sensitive to the issues that LGBTQ teens face, but if there were some genuine understanding, why would we have been paraded up here at the end of this show as some kind of exhibition?

I should have known when we entered the recreation center's gymnasium and saw the camera lights. At first I thought we were in the wrong place.

"No, you're right, baby, this is the open house," said the woman handing out pizza slices and grape drink. "You all just come on in here." Her gold-plated bracelets clinked and her curled hair extensions bounced as she handed each of us a Dixie cup filled with fizzy purple liquid. She flashed a warm smile as she ushered us in.

They were recording their weekly television show. Mark, the program's director, lit up when he saw Raheem and Christina. His eyes traveled up and down, taking in Raheem's overt attempts at passing as a straight black man: do-rag wrapped tightly around his head, baggy jeans sagging below his butt, a black hoodie hiding the white tank top underneath. But the vibrant blue contact lenses—and the way he taped his eyes back under his do-rag so they'd look what he calls "chinky"—overshadowed his attempts at blending in. Where Raheem pretended to want to go unnoticed, Christina was explicit, her candor and personality embodied by the one word that was used around Keap Street to describe the most admired residents: fierce. It was a cultivated position that most of the teens aspired to. Although the word was tossed around the house, overused, few of the residents lived out its meaning the way Christina did.

Only a few days earlier, she was swaggering around the house as if at a cocktail party, talking about her night out. "Denzel is so crazy," she said with a sigh. "I should give that boy a call. And J. Lo needs to step off. That bitch act like some kind of hooked-on-phonics off-the-boat queen. She needs to leave the ghetto *in* the ghetto. You know what I said to her? I said, 'That face is tired, OK Miss Thing?'" When the other residents told her she was dreaming, that she never met Denzel or J. Lo, Christina just shook her head and walked upstairs to her room. Minutes later, as I was getting ready to leave the house for the office, she sashayed into the living room, dropped two photographs on the coffee table, then continued on into the kitchen without even a pause. I picked up the photographs and examined them. One picture was of Christina smiling, standing next to Denzel Washington, who looked trapped, his face stern, his eyes angry. The other was of Christina next to a woman whose face was blurred, turning away from the camera. Although the image wasn't clear, when I looked closely there was no mistaking. It was Jennifer Lopez trying to get away from Christina.

Despite the winter chill, Christina dressed for the open house in a white halter top and skin-tight fuchsia pants. Her hair extensions were highlighted purple to complement her jeans. When we got out of the van and made our way up to the recreation center, Christina wobbled, her feet swimming in too-big white stiletto heels while trying to strut like the models she'd seen on TV. I had to plead with her to take off her sunglasses before entering the building even though the sun had set hours before.

Mark's smile was hidden under his mustache; he swallowed a few times before speaking.

"Are you from one of the gay group homes?" he asked.

Christina snapped her fingers in front of his face.

"Do the math," she said, and winked.

He asked if we'd like to be interviewed for the program. Christina didn't hesitate and agreed. Raheem was more reluctant. He had told me earlier that he wanted to talk exclusively to white families because, as he saw it, black people only fostered with the intent to adopt for money. I looked around. Mark and I were the only white people in the room. Jessica told me before I left not to expect much. Teenagers in the system are notoriously difficult to place in foster homes, and adoption is rare. The majority of foster parents are older, uneducated, and living in poverty. An adolescent, in the chaotic throes of puberty—combined with the trauma that comes with the abuse and neglect they've already experienced—is more than most foster parents are willing to take on. Add the LGBTQ component, and the odds diminish even more.

Youth in our program have said repeatedly that they've faced a continuous stream of rejection from previous foster parents. When the youth's sexual or gender identity is discovered, they get sent back to the agency, or they're berated and abused for their "sinful" lifestyle. Frequently, the homes the youth end up in are nearly as bad as the ones from which they were removed. The result is a series of retraumatizations, triggering already raw feelings of rejection.

After some needling from Christina, Raheem agreed to Mark's request for an interview. Maybe some white people would see him on TV, he reasoned. When Raheem seemed secure in his decision, I OK'ed it—assuming I'd sit in the back of the audience and watch.

"I'd like to have you up there too," Mark said.

I felt a pang of panic. The idea of sitting up there and being questioned about our program caused my own insecurities to surface. But I knew Raheem and Christina would never forgive me if I said no. I assured myself we'd be treated like all the others who sat in these chairs before us, the queer component discussed, of course, but not exploited.

"Can you tell us what that acronym stands for?" The voice echoes out into the gymnasium.

Although I'm sweating from the heat of the camera lights, I refuse to take off my baseball cap. "Lesbian, gay, bisexual, transgender, and questioning," I answer. I hear some of the teenagers who were up here moments before telling their stories of abandonment and abuse begin to snicker. None of their caseworkers move to quiet them.

Raheem sinks lower into his chair. He doesn't like his sexuality talked about on the streets, especially in black neighborhoods like Harlem. Coming here with Christina was difficult enough. He wouldn't walk anywhere near her, says she's too loud about it all, that she puts his sexuality "on blast." Suddenly I feel like I've made a mistake, as though I unwittingly marched them up onto an auction block. I want to grab them both by the wrists and run.

"Lesbian. Gay. Bisexual. Transgender. And questioning," he repeats slowly, as if considering the meaning of each word. I shift in my seat, notice that I'm drumming my fingers against the graffitied desk. I fold my hands under my armpits in order to stop. This open house is sponsored by an organization that tries to place teenagers in foster care with adoptive parents. Christina and Raheem were the only two residents from Keap Street who were interested in attending. They're also the least likely to be placed with adoptive parents.

Raheem is nineteen and just back in the program after a two-week stay in a psychiatric hospital in Queens. He agreed to go there after his third suicide attempt this year. The pattern is the same. He swallows a fistful of aspirin and calls Ms. Celeste—who he'd grown close to during a brief respite at the 401—from the apartment of his boyfriend, Tyrone. Ms. Celeste calls 911 while keeping him on the line, making sure he stays awake. From what I've gathered from conversations with co-workers, these attempts were never really viewed as serious efforts at taking his own life. The last time, however, he swallowed Tylenol P.M. and didn't call anyone. His boyfriend found him at the brink of consciousness, his limbs rubbery, the dark irises of his eyes rolled up inside his head. Raheem was rushed to the hospital, where he woke in the early morning, throwing up charcoal with Jessica and Gladyce at his bedside.

Even before I met Raheem I heard he had a reputation for trouble. The previous month he'd been sent to a different group home for a respite placement—a temporary change of residency. The program had to look out for the well-being of all the residents. Jessica had repeatedly made deals with Raheem, even having him sign a contract. When returning from the respite it was made clear he'd have to follow all program rules and regulations or an alternative placement would have to be found for him. No more attacking other residents or staff, no more destroying the house. Raheem had a habit of ripping apart the cable box and smashing the remote control if he couldn't watch the show he wanted. After a few weeks of behaving more or less appropriately, he came home past curfew covered in dirt, his elbows and knees scraped and bloody, his forehead badly bruised. Through tears and a shaking voice, he told staff he'd been accosted and raped walking home from the train. He was rushed to the hospital, given antibiotics to prevent STDs and an antiretroviral drug in hopes of stopping potential HIV infection. He met with a psychiatrist for evaluation and a psychologist for therapy. Within a few days Raheem seemed to have completely recovered, returning to his arrogant control over other residents. Finally someone squealed. The night he was allegedly raped Raheem had been seen rolling around on the sidewalk over by the abandoned movie theater on the corner, scratching his knees and arms against the cement, smacking his GED prep book against his head. When confronted by staff, he simply shrugged and confessed he had made the whole thing up because he'd been doing well and didn't want to get a level drop by coming in past curfew. The staff was horrified by how believable Raheem's performance was until Gladyce reminded everyone that he had plenty of real experience as a sexual abuse survivor to draw from.

When I came on as caseworker he was AWOL, living in Tyrone's place in the Brownsville section of Brooklyn—a two-bedroom apartment in the Howard Housing Projects that had been left to Tyrone by his mother when she moved down South. I heard from some of the other residents that the two of them were prostituting in order to pay the rent. Raheem's obsessive love for Tyrone, and Tyrone's eventually pulling away, became an obvious trigger for Raheem. He'd sink into despair and swallow pills, hoping that the fear of loss would recapture Tyrone's loyalty for at least a few more months.

It's not hard to understand Raheem's response to abandonment. When I asked him about his life before foster care he spoke about himself in the third person with a morose detachment, as if reciting a passage that he had memorized from his case file. His language mirrored the matter-of-fact social work vernacular heard at Service Plan Reviews—evidence of his time in care: "Raheem was born in an abandoned building. His father, for as far back as Raheem could remember, molested him. He wasn't allowed to go to school because his father feared that his own actions would be discovered by the outside world. Raheem's day-to-day routine included: home-schooling by his father, watching his mother get beat, then, when his father's not beating his mother, he would come for Raheem or even the family dog that Raheem's mother named Bitch."

Homeless shelters, squatting in abandoned buildings with his crack-addled parents, nights without light, days without heat: these were all parts of the story he told. Some details he changed. Raheem claimed he was eventually put in school by his godmother, an actress on his favorite soap opera, who used her address when signing him up so he'd be placed in her neighborhood district. I heard later from staff that he was only introduced to the actress through a charity event for marginalized children. He had embellished much of their history together, describing elaborate dinners at her Upper East Side apartment and weekend trips to the Hamptons, as if he studied her soap opera world and inserted himself into each scenario. In reality, he's rarely left the poorer, rundown neighborhoods of New York City.

Unlike Raheem, Christina occasionally makes it upstate, not for hikes in the Adirondacks but to a juvenile facility, remanded for prostituting or shoplifting. Institutions that incarcerate juveniles in New York State are notorious for many forms of violence. Allegations of physical assault and sexual abuse are common. Because these places don't recognize transgender identity as legitimate, Christina is forced to stay in the boy's wing. Feminizing hormones are considered contraband. All the transitioning toward womanhood that she's made up to this point is lost. Without estrogen she'll become more irritable and aggressive; she'll grow facial hair. Anything considered feminine by the staff will be stripped from Christina, including her fake hair and nails. They acknowledge her only by her birth name, Oscar. Now that she's older she knows how to carry herself when locked up, and fights back when being forced to go down on male residents or staff.

I don't understand fully what she's endured in detention because Christina rarely talks about herself. She'll prattle on and on about her nights out, her fabulous clothes, or Britney Spears's reality TV show, but not about anything beneath the surface. Most of the other residents eventually tell their story when trust is established. Not Christina. She wants to be seen as a starlet and distances herself from all the missteps recorded in her case file.

We were introduced last summer when I was still a residential counselor at the 401. We took the residents from both houses to Fire Island for a day at the beach, where they were surrounded by shiny, sunburned men clasping each other's hands, the throbbing and punishing moan of dance music radiating from bar speakers. Christina had just seen *Bridget Jones's Diary,* and while the other trans girls wore baggy swim trunks and tight bikini tops, Christina walked down the beach under the shade of her umbrella, her hair wrapped in a white towel, a shawl thrown over her shoulders. We walked past sandy dunes pushed up against the shingled beach homes and set up camp with blankets, handing out the cold-cut sandwiches and generic sodas. While Bella, Benny, and Rodrigo fought over the portable CD player—lip-synching their favorite songs—Christina found herself bored with the beach. She rose from her towel, shed her covering, and stood over me with the sun just over her shoulder. In the white glare I watched her adjusting her bikini top and fan off her skin beading with sweat. She looked toward the buildings that stood against the banks of sand.

"I must retire to the lavatory," she said.

I nodded and watched as she walked away, growing smaller in the distance until she moved off the boardwalk and into the shaded brush, where she knew men would be lurking. When she returned a half hour later her face was all flush and alive, the boredom washed clean. She poked Benny who was baking on his towel.

"We just must go for a stroll, dear boy," she said, waving a twenty-dollar bill at him. She had Bridget Jones sounding like a fey Sherlock Holmes. Benny sat up on one elbow, wiped the sweat from his eyes. "Where you get that money?" he asked. She pulled away and folded her arms around her waist.

"You don't want to go, fine," she said, breaking character, and began to walk off.

Bella got up from her towel. "I'ma go with you." I called after them, asking if they wanted to pick the music we were playing, trying to convince them to stay with the group, but they refused. She said they'd find us before we headed home.

Just as I was trying to get to know Christina, she was sent away again. Shortly after the trip to Fire Island she was remanded back upstate to an Office of Children and Family Services residential treatment center after another incident in Manhattan. I found out from Jessica that Christina had become involved with a professional boxer who had a penchant for trans girls. This guy, who supposedly hung out in Mike Tyson's camp, would pick up Christina off the stretch of the West Side Highway where she'd regularly stroll. They'd make their way to a hotel, where he'd drink down a bottle of Hennessy in order to release the asphyxiating grip of his inhibitions. But on this night there was no hotel, the boxer too drunk to make it to the lobby steps. Somehow they stumbled into Union Square Park. He passed out cold under a tree while trying to undo his zipper. When Christina realized he wasn't coming to, she removed his pants and made her way toward Broadway with his American Express Platinum card zipped up securely in her purse. She dumped his pants in a trashcan a few blocks away.

By the time the boxer woke up, a few thousand dollars had been charged to his card. He must have gone to the piers and asked where Christina lived, because the next day he showed up at Keap Street with his crew. Four hulking men poured out of a black SUV, pounded on the group home door, and demanded she man up. Staff barricaded the door while the residents pelted the men with food from the second-story windows. Only after Octavia screamed that the police were on the way did they leave. I guess the boxer didn't feel like explaining to the cops how a "tranny" left him in the park penniless, wearing only his underwear. This incident resulted in Christina being sent upstate in an emergency placement.

Her tendency is to forget, if not to erase. When she's not locked up she does just that every day, stripping away the boy she was raised to be and reinventing herself, trying on personalities like she would shoes, attempting to find the perfect fit for the young woman she will become.

Her case file is vague. Her parents are both dead. She has a maternal aunt somewhere in the city who refuses to accept Christina's transgender identity. A younger sister is out there somewhere in the system as well, but her name and placement are nowhere to be found. I've learned through co-workers that Christina's father was involved in a gang, most likely the Latin Kings. When she was younger an altercation broke out in their apartment and her father was shot. He bled to death on the floor in front of her as her mother wailed for help. A few years later her mother died from AIDS complications. Christina lived with her aunt until she was thrown out at the age of thirteen. In a rare moment of vulnerability she shared with staff her aunt's reasoning: no faggot is going to live under this roof, she was told.

"Some people watching at home or in the audience might be wondering why there needs to be a group home especially for gay kids," the voice says. "Would you care to explain?" I can feel myself getting defensive, worried that the commentator will try to parse anything I say, try to poke holes. I breathe deeply and tell myself it's just nerves. I'm aggravated because I haven't slept much. No one's attacking us here, I try to assure myself. The guy asking the questions is Mark, and Donald, the program's assistant director, is the cameraman. Before they started taping I watched Donald fiddle with the camera and the sound feeds. He limped from wall outlet to camera, sweating profusely, constantly wiping his forehead and the back of his neck with a frayed washrag he kept draped over his bald head.

When I mentioned the idea of going to the open house earlier that week, I was surprised by Raheem's reaction. He stood up off the couch and clapped his hands. A few years back he was set up with a possible match through the same program, organized by Donald. After Raheem missed three meetings, the potential adopter grew frustrated and decided to stop pursuing a relationship with him. I assumed he would want nothing to do with the program after that experience.

"The director dude will be there?" Raheem asked.

"Yeah, I think so."

"Oh, word? I want to go. Mos def," he said, beaming.

It wasn't until we arrived in Harlem and I saw Raheem's face drop when meeting the program's director that I understood. "*That's* Mark Steines?" Raheem asked. "I thought he'd be that dude from *Entertainment Tonight*." The gymnasium is quiet now except for the restless kids who have finished their pizza and the whine of folding chairs under fidgeting caseworkers. I answer Mark's question about the need for our home by saying that in addition to the neglect, abuse, or abandonment that brings all kids into foster care, LGBTQ youth endure a lot of additional obstacles. I quote statistics I've committed to memory, counting out each point on my fingers.

"Forty percent of gay teens said they were forced into sexual contact against their will, compared to 8 percent in the overall population. Gay teens are more likely to abuse alcohol and drugs and more frequently." Someone's cellphone goes off. The ring tone is "My Humps" by the Black Eyed Peas and a few kids start up, hollering, "What you gonna do with all that junk? All that junk inside your trunk? I'ma get, get, get, get you drunk, get you drunk off my hump." The room explodes into laughter. Mark and Donald shush them until they settle down.

Although it feels pointless, I go on, and note that despite what many people think, gay teens are more likely to join a gang as a way to eliminate bullying. Unemployment in the trans community is four times the national average.[1] As a result, many teens resort to sex work in order to survive. Another report indicates that gay, lesbian, and transgender youth are at least twice as likely to attempt suicide as their straight peers.[2] I tell the audience that queer kids experience homophobia and transphobia on the street, in school, and at work. Most group homes aren't equipped to provide the same type of security for LGBTQ youth as they do for straight youth. Many of our young people report that when living in a general-population group home they encounter harassment, ridicule, or physical or sexual assault on a daily basis. The program's goal is to provide a safe place for them to be themselves. They experience enough hatred in their everyday lives; they shouldn't have to face that at home as well.

Christina gives me little guttural affirmations as I talk, a kind of under-the-breath amen. Raheem sits up slightly, his finger traces the black cord of the microphone. I'm surprised by my response, that I'm able to keep myself so composed while my nerves make me feel as if I'm about to unravel. I notice my hand trembling slightly as I hold the microphone. Raheem grabs it from me and slides it in front of himself, leans close, almost pressing his lips against it. He pauses, his breath amplified throughout the room.

"This program," he says. "This program is the only home I ever really had."

Raheem stares down at the desk.

"When I was little I had nothing. Got beat a lot. I lived in like nine foster homes and got beat there too. This one place, right? They just locked me up in a closet when they left out of the house because they said they didn't trust no faggot," he says. "I didn't even get to eat the same food their real kids ate." He talks about why our program is so important.

"So at Keap Street it's like we got a place, you know what I'm saying? We go on recreation and that's wassup. We went to that one poetry place. How you call it? Oh, and that camping trip. Yo, get this, they took us—yo, Ryan, where you take us?—someplace like out in the woods with the bugs and we had to *sleep* out there in tents. No bathrooms around. No joke. Yo, let me tell you, that was mad crazy. You hear like bears growling and killing goats and shit. Sorry, and stuff, I mean. They got us doing things we wouldn't normally do. That's what I'm taking about. The program's mad cool and all that but I want a family, you know? I always be thinking about that. Like coming home after school and having a snack with my new mom and I'd have my own room. We'd do things, you know, things families do."

He's captured the room's attention. The chairs stop moaning under the shifting weight of bored caseworkers and the kids stop whispering. I've never seen this kind of energy from Raheem except when he talks about Tyrone. This is the impassioned, brilliant Raheem. Not chained to depression, not seized by his tangled past. He's advocating for himself in a way no one else can. His firsthand experience rings truer than my calculated caseworker-speak ever could.

But then he falters, slips into histrionics, embellishes grades, fabricates IQ tests, makes up jobs modeling and dancing. His body straightens up and he clasps the microphone in his hand like a pop singer.

"I been through it, yo," he says. "But I still do me. That's why I'm pursuing a career in modeling. I'm in talks with Sean John right now."

I watch as he begins to create himself in front of this audience, molding the jagged corners of his life into something smooth, something remarkable. Replacing whatever feels ordinary with the extraordinary until he resembles the perfect adolescent son. The one they want; the one they'll take home, different from the kid who was hauled away by cops for assaulting another resident or threatening to attack a staff member with a kitchen chair. When he tells the audience about helping a timid new resident adjust to the group home, he leaves out that it was a ploy to get the boy in the basement bathroom for his initiation.

Not to be outdone, Christina reaches over me and grabs the microphone from Raheem, flips her hair back, and begins to speak in the southern drawl she's been perfecting the past few weeks, ever since Britney's television show aired. Her words sparrow from her mouth, clipping the end of each phrase. She says she wants a family to take her in that can provide for her, show her she's loved, and help her succeed in life as a famous singer.

"I'm supposed to be meeting a record producer real soon," she says. She begins to describe herself, her sisterly love for Britney, their shared affection for tennis and strawberry Frappuccinos. Her body rises from her seat when she talks about her driver's license test and doing hair at the salon. If this was a radio show you might think you were listening to a teenager from Baton Rouge, not the South Bronx.

They raise the lights in the gymnasium so the audience can ask us questions. There's an awkward silence. Some of the kids are tilting back in their folding chairs, balancing on the rear two legs. The night has been long and everyone wants to go home. But one man is peering up at us who seems interested and wants to know more. He's sitting in the middle of the crowd, his bald, black head hovering above like an orb. He's wearing a T-shirt with Bugs Bunny sporting bling and toting a gun. The bald guy raises his hand, looks over to Mark, then to Raheem.

"I really feel what you been talking about," he says. Even though he's seated away from us I can hear a thick, smoker's wheeze when he inhales. "I'm looking to adopt if I find the right match," his eyes raise and focus on Raheem. "And I just wanted to ask some questions if you don't mind." How do they feel about chores? Do they help around the house, he wants to know. Curfew is something that must be followed. Do they come home on time at the group home? What about cooking? Do they keep their rooms clean now?

A few people get up, walk to the pizza boxes and bottles of soda. When they see everything is gone they walk out, the door screeches shut behind them. Raheem and Christina are both nodding their heads to the bald man's questions.

"Yeah," Raheem says. "We got to do chores at the house. We got to follow the rules, you know?" According to Christina they both come in at curfew, keep their rooms clean, even help with cooking. These revisions are seamless; the acumen, quick. They don't blink or misstep, giving the man exactly what he wants to hear without sounding too perfect. Raheem says with a self-effacing smile, "I don't really like to do dishes but I can learn."

When an elderly woman asks Christina if she can follow instruction she tosses her hair around, does her best Britney. "*Moi?*" she asks, wide-eyed, her hand fanned across her chest. She throws her head back and laughs. The remaining members of the audience, not quite sure what to do, laugh with her. I think about the time Christina acquired a pair of handcuffs and plotted a scheme that would eventually land her upstate. She and a few other trans girls went on the stroll in the Meatpacking District, leading a john into a more secluded area. When he offered money, they flipped the script, pretending to be undercover cops, and slapped the handcuffs on him.

When he was sufficiently restrained, the girls besieged him, beat him, and stole his wallet. They tried their luck a second time, but the ruse didn't hold. They were busted and sent upstate to a juvenile facility.

I look at Raheem and Christina. In this moment they are becoming who they have to be in order to get what they need. With ingratiating finesse they work the crowd, and I watch them do what has kept them barely afloat in life, allowing them to survive on the street. They do whatever it takes to hold the attention of this audience, because life has shown them that being themselves is never enough.

Reinvention is a large part of black and brown queer youth culture in New York. Raheem and Christina both attend the balls where voguing sprang up. (The dance, characterized by model-inspired poses and sharp movements, was later appropriated and popularized by Madonna.) Groups, known as "houses," gather at all-night parties where members of each house perform in competitions demonstrating their skills for passing as someone else. The competitors "walk" in different categories: Realness with a Twist, Wall Street Executive Realness, Super Model Realness, Construction Worker Realness. The houses also function as families. For those who were abandoned, kicked out, or orphaned, the "House Mother," often a transwoman, is there to provide guidance in all things competitive and personal.

In the gym, the bald guy raises his hand again; Mark calls on him.

"What about allowance? You get money for doing chores now?"

"If you follow the rules at the house and do chores you get allowance. But it ain't nothing," Christina says, scowling at me. The audience laughs. Then she says how money doesn't really matter to her. Raheem nods, agrees.

"I don't really need too much," she says, dressed in her stolen Juicy Couture, brushing away the idea with her hand. "Most trans girls trick for money, honey, almost everybody does it, but not me. I got too much self-respect. I'm paying it, honey." "Paying it," a term I've become accustomed to hearing, is the queer youth equivalent of "sucking it up" when things get difficult.

Raheem nods. "I ain't throwing shade at nobody," he says, "but a lot of gay boys sell it for the cheddar. I don't play like that."

For a moment I feel obligated to object, call them out on all their lies, but I don't. One thing I understand about Keap Street is why residents constantly repackage themselves. Nothing makes more sense to me than Christina's southern charm or Raheem's soap opera godmother. They are rewriting certain parts of their lives in order to hide others. I don't interrupt their tales of good behavior and good graces. The crowd is clearly willing to believe. I glance in the direction of the glaring camera lights, into the black eye of the lens and think, For those of you watching at home, what you're now witnessing is the hustle.

The bald man keeps raising his hand, waving it around. He's asking questions but looks like he already knows all the answers. I don't like how he's looking at Raheem or the heat in his tone when he speaks.

"Would you be able to live outside of the city? Me, for example, I live in the North Bronx. There's no trains around me. So I guess I'm asking if you would live far from the city." All the gush of flirtation is there. He's edging up to the end of his seat, his hands now clasped as his elbows rest on his knees.

"I could live anywhere as long as it's safe and friendly," Raheem says. Christina and I look over at Raheem at the same time. Christina shakes her head then pulls out her compact and fixes her lipstick.

The bald guy, still looking at Raheem, says, "I know what it's like not to be cared about. I'm not somebody who disappears. I want to be that parent that's always there."

A few weeks before Raheem's mother died, we received a call from a social worker at Brookdale Hospital. She wanted Raheem to know his mother's situation had taken a turn for the worse. "If he wants to say goodbye, now's the time." Raheem's father had passed away the month before, and everyone at Keap Street was concerned about his cold and flippant response. He didn't want to talk about anything, stopped showing up to his mandatory therapy appointments with Laura, dropped out of his GED classes, and spent long hours, sometimes days, away from the program. When he was at the house he alienated himself from the other residents with his violent eruptions and erratic swings of emotion. Staff tried to engage him but there was nothing to discuss as far as Raheem was concerned. His father died. End of story.

Raheem's relationship with his mother was different. They suffered many of the same abuses and shared a bond regardless of their estrangement. Staff knew Raheem would be deeply affected if his mother died, especially if he never had an opportunity to make peace. Many of us were afraid that his mother's failing health could drive Raheem further into himself, isolating him even more from help, or perhaps trigger the violent behaviors that we had been working so hard to help him control. Another suicide attempt was the true fear on everyone's mind, but this time we knew he wouldn't simply toy with aspirin. Gena stopped by Keap Street that afternoon unannounced to tell him about his mother's condition and to see if he could be persuaded to make a trip to the hospital.

Raheem was still in bed. He had come home at around five in the morning "dazed and tired," according to the logbook. Gena walked into his room and found him on his stomach burrowed under his SpongeBob comforter. There were no sheets on his mattress, only the mandatory plastic covering. His feet hung over the end, the bottoms of his white socks shaded with dirt. His legs bucked up to his belly and then pushed out into a trembling stretch. His arms lifted overhead as he let out a yawn.

"Long night?"

Raheem rolled over and looked at her. His blue contact lenses weren't in. Foreign, brown eyes stared up. A stretch of skin near his temples was discolored and scarred from where he taped back his eyes. Gena said that she had something important to discuss and that she'd wait for him to wake up before they talked.

When they got to the hospital his mother was propped up and asleep in bed. They both stopped at the sight of her. Gena said she was frail. Her thin arms twitched as she battled something in her dreams. Her head hung down and her eyes were half-closed. Her breathing, rough and ragged, cut through the static silence of the room. AIDS had ravaged her. Raheem stayed near the door as Gena made her way in and sat on the bed next to her. The curtains were drawn and flashes of light splashed against her body from the muted TV.

"Come over here, Raheem," Gena said. "You want to sit down?"

"No," he said, looking up at the stencil trim on the wall. "I want to go. Can we go?" According to Gena their voices must have roused his mother because she gasped, her eyes opened wide. She looked out blankly, unable to find them.

"Raheem, you want to say hi to your mother?" Gena asked, looking back at him. He moved in closer with wary, slow steps. When he made his way to the foot of the bed he stopped and looked toward the window.

"Hi," he said.

Gena described his mother as balding, with wiry black hair curling from her chin and cheeks. A lump the size of a baseball pressed out of one side of her neck. Gena placed her hand against Raheem's mother's arm and her fingers sunk in as if touching bruised fruit. Tubes spliced into her veins; the monitor overhead let out a measured, tinny beep.

"She don't look right," Raheem said, brushing away tears.

"Do you want to sit down with her?" Gena asked, gesturing to the other side of the bed. He moved cautiously over to her and sat across from Gena. Then suddenly the woman's eyes flashed around the room.

"We're right here," Gena answered, rubbing her thumb on the woman's arm. "Raheem's here with you." She continued to search around as if she didn't hear Gena. Her mouth, mostly toothless, was open and her eyes looked startled. A string of saliva began to drip from her lips and collected in a growing pool on her hospital gown. A crackling wheeze came from the back of her throat. Gena said she grabbed a piece of paper towel off the tray and dabbed the saliva from her chin. Raheem stared quietly as if trying to find his mother somewhere in the features of this woman's face.

"She look so old," he said, shaking his head. "How she get to look so old?"

Gena reached across his mother and took Raheem's hand in her own, pushing the paper towel in his palm, and raised it up to his mother's face. Gena said they wiped her lips and chin together until gradually Gena pulled away. Raheem's hand stayed pressed against the weathered skin of his mother's cheek.

"I'll just be outside," Gena said, standing up, inching out of the room. "Raheem, now's the time to say what you need to say to your mother."

His shoulders shook as she closed the door behind her.

"Oh, Mama" is all she heard.

We walk out of the gymnasium and on to 125th Street, where the artist De La Vega has chalked a message onto the sidewalk: "This moment is more precious than you think." The wind whips around and slaps our faces. I curl from the impact and nestle my chin into my chest. I expect Raheem and Christina to complain about how "brick" it is outside but they seem unaffected by the cold, bouncing along with all the possibility the interview has brought them. They're in front of me as I pat down my pockets, trying to find my cigarettes. Normally I don't smoke in front of the youth I work with, but I'm especially annoyed and can't wait the hour it'll take to drop them off at Keap Street. I use them as a shield from the wind and light my cigarette.

"Hey, wait up," a voice calls out behind us. We turn around to find the bald guy jogging toward us. He's much larger now that he's standing, a full head taller than me. He reaches into his pocket and pulls out a pack of Newports, slides one into his mouth. "Got a light?" We pause on the corner of 125th and Lenox Avenue as I hand over my matches. Christina is twirling, humming a song. Raheem is posing with his legs spread wide. He unzips his hoodie and hooks his thumbs into his jeans pockets, pulling at his waistband and exposing his boxers. He licks his lips, wears a disaffected pout. His body is rigid and I can tell he's flexing.

"My name's Clarence," the man says, lifting his head and blowing a cloud of smoke that escapes into a gust of wind. He looks to Raheem. "You mentioned you're a dancer. I am too. Well, back in the day I was." He shakes his ass a little and winks. "Now I do interior design." I watch him watch Raheem, the way his eyes look up and down, admiring.

"Oh, yeah?" Raheem says, allowing the corners of his mouth to turn up. "That's mad cool."

"I was really digging what you were saying in there," Clarence says and gestures back to the recreation center. "Young brothers need a role model. You know what I'm saying?" Christina has now turned her back to the conversation; this attention on Raheem is apparently too much to bear.

"Maybe you want to come to my place this weekend," Clarence says. "I'm having some friends over for a barbeque." I flick my cigarette out to the curb before I'm finished and push my hands into my pockets. A barbeque? In January?

"Clarence, I think a neutral space would be more appropriate for a first meeting," I say. He nods his head without taking his eyes off Raheem.

"Give a brother your number," Clarence says to him and takes out his cellphone. I take a step closer and try to cut into his line of vision.

"If you're interested in meeting up with Raheem you can call my office number and I'll see if I can set something up," I say and nudge Christina and Raheem in the direction of the van.

"Yo, Raheem, we should most definitely meet up," Clarence says, and continues to walk with us. "We a good match."

"That's wassup," Raheem says, casually lifting his shirt, exposing a slice of his belly. When we get to the van I unlock the doors and tell them both to get in. Clarence asks how I can be reached.

"Call my office," I say. For a moment I think of giving him a fake number but instead offer up the general information line. "They'll put you in touch with me." I get into the van and pull away. Clarence grows smaller and smaller in the rearview mirror, continuing to wave at us from the curb until I turn out of view.

Christina and Raheem are high from the interview and all the attention.

"We going to be on TV," she says, looking through the windshield, which reflects a constellation of streetlights. "Strictly red carpet from here on out." She snaps her fingers, snaps her head into a vogue pose, her hair tumbling around her.

"Think of all the calls we going to get," Raheem says. He does a little dance in his seat. "You think some white people watched, Ryan?"

I pull onto the FDR, merge into the artery of traffic.

"The show will play throughout Brooklyn," I say. "So probably."

There's a soft glow in the clouds above the city. Traffic is light. We'll get back sooner than I thought. Raheem stares out at the passing buildings, his forehead pressing against the window. He taps the glass separating him from the world just outside.

"That guy really likes me," he says. His fingertips press against their reflection. "Wonder if he's going to be my new Daddy."

CHAPTER 7

FIRE STARTER

I'm standing on an elevated subway platform with my head tilted back, staring up at a cloudless Brooklyn sky, trying to will away the clank of the approaching train. I breathe in deep, hoping to shut out the city noise a moment longer in order to settle my nerves, my stomach. Maite is standing next to me, splitting sunflower seeds between her teeth and spitting the shells at our feet.

"We eating soon? I'm mad hungry," she says.

There's a guy on the platform whose earphones are emitting loud, crashing beats. A young girl yells into her cellphone about her lame-ass boyfriend. A young mother tries to comfort her squalling child. The train screeches around the last bend before entering the station, staring us down with its ominous, glowing eyes. Pigeons flutter, scatter, then regroup. I breathe deep; return my focus to the sky.

We're late for our appointment to Maite's new school, which only adds to my aggravation. I called Keap

Street the previous night to make sure the house staff were aware of her appointment. I spoke to a new residential counselor named Sophia. I told her to wake Maite up at six, get her showered and fed, and have her prepared to leave the house when I arrived at seven. Be sure to write it in the log, I said, so there won't be any confusion when the staff switch over.

When I arrived at Keap Street this morning the house was in an uproar. Octavia had discovered that the safe was broken into overnight and a thousand dollars in petty cash and Metro cards were stolen. Fasheema, Bella, and Raheem were all AWOL at the time, which looked suspicious. When I found a gap in all the commotion, I asked if Maite was ready to go. The staff turned to me, silent.

"I called last night and spoke to Sophia," I said.

Octavia cleared her throat. "She didn't say nothing to me." She looked to her co-workers. "She didn't say nothing, right?" They both shook their heads. Octavia reached across the table for the log. "This ain't my fault." She thumbed to the previous night's entries, scanned the page until her eyes narrowed. "Oh, shit. Yeah, here it is. My bad. Sorry, Sugar."

Upstairs, Maite's room still carried the sweet odor of the weed she'd smoked out her window a few hours before. Octavia warned me that Maite wouldn't budge. "It'd take that girl two hours to watch *60 Minutes*," she scoffed. Maite rarely got out of bed for meetings

or appointments. Since coming to the program a few
months prior, she had demonstrated what clinicians call
a "chronic dependency" smoking weed. She can become
explosive with anger when not high and deflects her
emotions with superficial attachments. If something is
bothering her, and she's smoked that day, she disengages
completely. When she's had appointments in the past, the
staff have typically given her two warnings to get out of
bed before giving up. I've overheard some of the workers' conversations about how things would be different if
these were their own children, bolstered by the idea that
all these teens need is to have some sense knocked back
into them.

I tried using the tricks I learned from Ms. Celeste at
the 401 to get residents out of bed, but nothing worked
on Maite. Finally, I promised to buy her lunch at her
favorite Puerto Rican restaurant down the block if she got
up. She lazily acquiesced to my bribe. After a half-hour
shower and another forty-five minutes deciding what to
wear, she made her way out onto the street.

The train barrels into the station and we push onto a
crowded car. Maite makes her way for the one open seat,
just beating an elderly woman bearing in the same direction. The woman grumbles to herself but Maite doesn't
move, just spits sunflower seed shells in the woman's
direction.

"Maite," I hiss. "Get up."

She pretends not to hear me, puts on her head-
phones, closes her eyes, and starts singing a Janet Jack-
son song, loudly and off-key. I take a deep breath and
try to shut out Maite's disdain for everything, and the
judgment I feel coming from the commuters around me.
A woman pushes through the crowd, waving bright pam-
phlets overhead. "Find peace," she calls out. "You don't
have to be miserable. You can be saved."

My mind begins to crowd with the thoughts I've
been trying to ignore all morning: increasingly, I fear
there is little I'm capable of doing to help the youth in my
care. Within a system that paints in such broad strokes—
focusing more on warehousing youth than on providing connections to enable a successful life after aging
out—I feel there's little I can do to make a difference.
The bureaucracy is asphyxiating, and out of step with
the work foster care workers do. The powers that be seem
more concerned with documenting efforts to prove due
diligence around food and shelter than on helping young
people succeed. The burden of caring falls on workers
who find ways to show up for the youth despite the system's flaws. But being underpaid and overworked carries
its own burden. In my short time here I've seen workers
once beaming with enthusiasm become worn down and
discouraged by the limits of what's possible.

By the time Maite and I arrive at the school we're more
than two hours late. As I rummage for her paperwork—

the school records, state-issued identification, and birth certificate that I've spent the better part of two weeks trying to collect—I hear Maite at the security desk arguing with the guard about relinquishing her cellphone.

"I ain't handing over shit," she says, her phone clutched tight in her hand.

"You got to put it in this tray before walking through the metal detector," the guard answers. As they argue, she pulls out her cigarettes, lighter, and a small one-hitter used for smoking weed. The guard looks at me and lets me know this type of contraband isn't allowed in school.

I force a smile. "Of course not."

"Fine," Maite says. "Then I ain't going to school here."

"Maite . . . " But she's already stuffing her things back into her pockets and walking toward the door. Out on the sidewalk she lights a Newport and exhales smoke with an exasperated breath.

"You didn't even get through security," I say, following her.

"Fuck them."

"You have to go to school, you're sixteen."

"I don't have to do shit. I'll get my GED like everyone else."

I look at Maite, her furrowed brow, and feel like giving up. Despite all my preaching and pleading, most of the residents at Keap Street have dropped out of high school, the classroom environment proving too frustrating and antagonizing to handle. Already this semester I've been to two expulsion hearings because of residents fighting with other students. Truancy officers visit the home often, threatening an educational neglect charge against the agency. The residents argue that a GED is easier—why put up with the hassle of school?

I can't get Bella to focus on finding a place to live and she ages out of foster care in a month; Junior continues to live in a fantasy world, pretending to be a doctor; Christina is strolling more and more, staying out until the sun rises; theft is an epidemic in the house, and the program nurse told me the residents are passing gonorrhea around like it's going out of style. How can I manage such insurmountable problems when I can't even get Maite to attend her first day of school? Simple tasks that would take the average person no more than a week to achieve require a cascade of busywork, taking months to accomplish. If a resident has to get a state-issued ID, I have to be methodical about coordinating the house staff and the resident to meet this goal—calling at every shift change to make sure it's been communicated to the incoming staff—or else the resident won't be home for the appointment. If a Social Security card is issued, the resident will insist on holding on to it, and inevitably—before I can make a copy for our records—it's lost.

Three steps back accompany any tiny stride forward. My struggle against the residents' combative pasts, and an antiquated bureaucracy masquerading as support, feels like a losing battle. But I muster up enough resolve to at least point out the obvious to Maite.

"We need to have a discussion about this," I say. "Your education is important."

She isn't listening. She stares at a billboard on a passing bus. "You seen that movie, *Hustle and Flow*? That shit look mad cool."

I arrive at the office a little before noon after my early lunch with Maite. Just as I'm putting down my bag, Jessica walks into my cubicle and tells me I missed court today for Junior. It's not my fault, I'm assured, as I was never informed of the hearing. The court has rescheduled. I'll need to be there with a report.

"Write this down," she says. I grab a legal pad and a pen.

"Manhattan Family Court, Part 49. The DLS attorney is Ms. Holden and the law guardian is Ms. Blake. You need to follow up. Also, the social worker from Julio's school called this morning. His mother changed the locks on him yesterday and he had to sleep in the park last night. The trial discharge obviously isn't working. Find him a respite bed to stay in temporarily. Also, your UCRs are due to ACS in this order in two weeks." She hands me a sheet of paper with six residents' names. A UCR is a long, detailed report—the written version of a Service Plan Review—completed for each youth every six months.

"Start with Caridad and work your way down. And before the weekend you'll need to do a home assessment at Manny's mom's." She pauses, smiles. "Good morning."

Officially, I'm supposed to have monthly face-to-face contact with the parents of the twelve youth in my care. I'm mandated to have weekly contact with all the residents. Every six months, I hold formal Service Plan Reviews for each youth. The family, the youth, and their law guardians and agency workers are encouraged to attend to re-evaluate the living arrangement and progress of the youth. In addition, I go to court with them for their twice-annual permanency hearings. Hypothetically I can be in court or a meeting more than once a week, attempting to visit the family a few days every week, and inscribing substantial paperwork for each encounter or attempted encounter. The rest of the time I try to piece together a few minutes here and there with the youth, check in on their daily progress, and build our relationship.

I'd been planning to return to Keap Street after getting some paperwork done, check in with Maite after our school mishap this morning, and see if I could have some face time with Junior. Staff have complained he's been elusive lately. They think he's dating an older man and that's why he's rarely around. Last week Junior pulled up to Keap Street driving a gray BMW convertible, honking the horn. Gladyce tried to impress upon him that driving someone else's car, no matter how he obtained it, without a license as an undocumented immigrant could unleash a levee of problems for his immigration case. He seemed unmoved by her speech. She asked if I could try to talk some sense into him.

As I'm combing through my pile of work, the phone rings. When I answer, Gladyce's voice comes through the receiver with the force of a hurled brick.

"Well, shit gone and hit the fan today," I hear her say, and my stomach tightens. She informs me that Fasheema and Raheem returned to Keap Street after going AWOL with new tattoos and new clothes. "Looks like we got our thieves. And if that ain't enough, Maite just set the second floor bathroom on fire."

Gladyce tells me that Steve found Maite's stash of weed, a plentiful amount, and flushed it down the toilet. When Maite returned home after our morning excursion, she caught wind of this and became enraged, railing uncontrollably. She cornered Steve, slammed him into the door, knocking the wind out of him. She then locked herself in the bathroom. Moments later, thick smoke began to billow from under the door. When she came rushing out, coughing, the shower curtain was ablaze, flames rising up the wall. The fire department was called and Maite had to be restrained. Gladyce took her to a psychiatric hospital for a full screening.

I'm asked to contact a pyromania specialist and have Maite evaluated. Gladyce seems to sense something in my silence and asks what's wrong.

"It's just been a hard day," I say dismissively. "I'm feeling overwhelmed." What I don't say is that I'm afraid I'm experiencing burnout, and because little evidence of improvement is apparent in the youth, I fear what social workers call "compassion fatigue" may soon follow.

"Junior giving you attitude? You can't let these kids do you like that. You need to know how to detach. Look at me for example." I imagine her in her orange lipstick and orange shirt that matches her orange shoes. "When the day is done. It. Is. Done. You let go." She clears her throat and talks a bit lower. "Check out a little early today. Get yourself to a bar and release whatever child's life is putting your mind to worry."

"I can't. I have clinical supervision with Laura."

I hear a voice in the background I don't recognize ask Gladyce why I can't go out.

"Fuck clinical supervision," the voice says. "He needs a clinical 'wussup' and beer supervision with peers."

After hanging up, I allow myself to consider what's happened to Maite. If I'd tried harder this morning, made more of an effort to get her into school, to understand what was behind her aversion, I'm convinced this incident could have been avoided. I don't know much about Maite's story. The things she's told me—her rich aunt and uncle in New Rochelle drive a Range Rover, her brother is in Iraq—don't stray past the surface. She hasn't opened up to me about what brought her to the group home, and I've been so harried with the needs of the other residents, I haven't taken the time to ask. I go to the cabinet and pull Maite's case file. In it is a vague history of "severe neglect and abuse," a drug-addicted mother who died from an overdose, a father who is listed as "unknown" but is rumored to have been murdered in a gang dispute. Her older siblings managed to find successful routes out of their messy situations. But Maite moved in with her aunt, the only family contact the agency has, briefly after her mother's death. There, her uncle constantly ridiculed her for being a lesbian, for not being "woman enough." Now her aunt has distanced herself after allegations that her husband sexually abused Maite.

I think about the fire Maite set, about what could have unleashed such fury inside her. The one thing she feels that gives her some authority over her life was taken away. Smoking weed allows her relief, commandeering the pain and loneliness she feels. She's found a way to wall herself off from what seems so lost. Who am I to tell her she needs to stop?

When I meet with Laura for clinical supervision, we talk about my recent home visit to Maite's aunt's house. After her assessment, Maite was placed in the psychiatric hospital for evaluation. There she became obsessed with returning to her family's fold, asking for me to set up a meeting. The place was just as Maite described. A large ranch-style house in New Rochelle, just north of the city, with a massive backyard and a Range Rover parked in the driveway.

Maite's aunt answered the door and revealed a living room scantly decorated, an enormous chandelier hanging over the entryway, and a few boxes stacked high in the corner. Her Bronx accent was thick, and I assumed they'd recently relocated. I was surprised to hear they'd been there for five years. Over the mantel was an enormous portrait of Maite's aunt and uncle at their wedding. In it, his large hands grip her hips as he presses his crotch into her. I was led into what she called the greenhouse, a back porch with a few potted plants on the floor. I learned her husband works as a maintenance man part time and that she stays home with Maite's sister's baby. This lifestyle, the house, the Range Rover, seemed suspiciously beyond the income of a part-time maintenance man.

When Maite's aunt went into her room to attend to the crying baby I wandered downstairs. The room was cool and dark. There was a small TV with a rabbit-ear antenna resting on a TV tray, and the board game Candy Land was splayed open on the linoleum floor. I glanced into an adjoining room where two single beds were situated next to each other. The room was gloomy, empty expect for a naked Barbie twisted into a frozen contortion in the corner, her hair chopped off, her hands mangled and burned. Next to her, a small bowl of dry cereal. When I turned around to make my way back upstairs I was startled by a young girl watching me in the hallway.

"Hi," I said.

She didn't respond. A mess of knotted blond hair obscured her face. Her small, pale legs fidgeted as she pulled at the oversized Mountain Dew T-shirt that hung from her like a dress. We stared at each other until Maite's aunt came downstairs with the baby in her arms.

"I see you met Violet, my foster child."

The little girl seemed shell-shocked. Looking at her, I couldn't help thinking of Maite's allegation of molestation. I asked the aunt if I'd get the chance to meet her husband. She averted her eyes and said he was working. The point of doing home visits is to determine if the environment is safe for a child to stay. Although the physical needs required for the foster child were accounted for—food, shelter—her emotional needs seemed clearly unmet. Nothing felt safe in their house, but there were no concrete indicators of abuse or neglect that I could point to, only a suspicion. All I could do was hunt down the girl's caseworker and let her know about Maite's accusation.

I can't grant Maite permission for a home visit, not that her aunt wanted her there anyway. She made it clear her niece wasn't welcome. I'm not sure how to break the news to Maite. I tell Laura that I can't help thinking that being jostled from one placement to another only exacerbates Maite's sense of abandonment. I'm concerned she'll return from the psychiatric hospital more alienated than before.

"And why do you feel that to be true?" she asks me.

"Maite has lived her whole life feeling her needs didn't matter, that she wasn't important enough to be loved. I'm afraid she'll see her removal from Keap Street as another rejection, another indication that how she feels isn't important. She hasn't been given enough time at one placement to make any real connections. And now it seems she shuts down if anyone tries." Laura looks at me intently. "Trust is a real issue for her," I say, and then look away.

Laura smiles. "You have good instincts and the residents are drawn to you. Believe in yourself a little more." This encouragement, coming from someone who has worked her whole adult life as a therapist, brings a wave of relief over me. Both she and Jessica carry a quiet wisdom about this work that I admire, especially as I'm faced with frustrations from what increasingly feels like a broken system.

"She's been shuffled around a lot, looked over. I don't think she's been given an opportunity to understand emotionally what's happened to her. Before she knows it, she's shipped off to another placement. I think that's affected her ability to function well." I continue, "She carries herself well on the street, but in reality she can't even get herself out of bed without staff helping her."

"Being abandoned at a young age results in the neglect of our development dependency needs. This is the major factor in why Maite—and so many of our residents—act out more than average teenagers," Laura says. "They're growing physically, intellectually, but emotionally, they're stunted." They grow up, and look like adults. Maite walks the walk and talks the talk, but beneath the surface is a person whose needs are insatiable because they weren't met as a child. "This longing," she notes, "is the core of compulsive and addictive behavior."

I think about Maite's incessant need to smoke weed, and how, to finance her habit, she began meeting up with a Pakistani boy down the block from Keap Street. He works at the bodega and gives her free weed, loosies, and Snapple in exchange for oral sex. She confessed in moments of desperation that she's considered getting pregnant. In her mind, she sees it as a way out of foster care, where she'll finally have someone who won't leave her. In reality, pregnancy would only further entrench her into foster care, placing her in a group home for mothers and their children, and most likely create a lifelong dependency on the system.

I leave my meeting with Laura and try to ignore the nagging sense that what we can provide Maite is so limited.

The sense of security we pretend to offer is superficial, and the reality, the scarcity of protection, feels morally criminal.

Maite looks calm, smiles at me in her teal hospital gown. Her hair is pulled back revealing clouded, peppercorn eyes. She's been at the psychiatric hospital for two weeks and is about to be released back into our care. I've come to talk with her, help her transition back into life at Keap Street. She only wants to hear about my home visit with her aunt. She's determined to return to the clutch of her family, regardless of how badly she was treated there. The allegations of sexual abuse by her uncle seem to wane from her memory. No charges were ever filed against the man. Maite said no one believed her.

I tell her that because of the allegations in her file, an agency-approved home visit with them isn't possible. Her face drops and she quickly revises her story. She shoves the memories of abuse out of her head and says they never happened. I want to tell her that her happiness can't be contingent on the acceptance of her family. It's heartbreaking to know that she's so desperate she'd rather return to that kind of abuse than continue in foster care. Her face is expressionless and her eyes are empty as she refuses to look at me.

The Maite I imagine fights against her shame, her abuse.

She's a young girl sitting up in bed, in the darkness, waiting. Every creeping sound shooting panic up her spine. Although the hot summer night fills her room, she has her blanket pulled up over her head. Through the gaps in the fabric, she watches the light at the bottom of her door, how it flickers with his passing footsteps. Disappear, she says to herself. Disappear. She holds her breath when her uncle walks in, creeping quietly to her, pressing his finger to her lips. This is the only way, he says, she's going to learn to act more like a lady.

The Maite I imagine rises above the clutch of this crime, past the reach and consequences of her uncle's brutality. She's able to understand she deserves to be loved despite what she's experienced.

I grab her hand and tell her that returning to Keap Street will be a new beginning. I try to get her excited about school, about meeting her goals, but her face remains expressionless. I try to remain optimistic for Maite, tell her this is a new opportunity to do better, but I can tell by her eyes that she sees my talk as naïve, wishful thinking.

The cafeteria bell rings. We sit in silence until her chin dimples. She then leans her head into my shoulder. I rub her back.

"I'm alone," she says, and her chest heaves.

"No. No, you're not," I hear myself say, wanting to believe it's true.

CHAPTER 8
DISAPPEAR

"You gonna quit?" Gladyce asks me as I sit on the front stoop of Keap Street, trying to light my cigarette.

"You smoke too," I say, and she fans her hair back, pointing her chin skyward. She pulls out a Virginia Slim on cue and holds it out, posing.

"But I look good. You look like a hot mess."

We're waiting for Bella to come downstairs. After much scrambling we finally found her a bed at a detox center. We have an appointment with the case manager. If all goes well, she'll have a place to go after aging out. If only we can get her there. Bella seemed to panic after Raheem said to her, "They going to tell you to hurry up and blow out the candles on your birthday cake so they can drop you off at your next destination."

After waiting for a half hour, we go inside to see what's the holdup. Gladyce knocks on the door to her room. We're met with silence.

"Come on, Bella. We got to do this now. No point in dragging this out." Nothing.

We announce that we are entering the room and find it empty. The window leading out to the fire escape is open, the venetian blinds drawn up to a tilted angle, and swaying. Bella's fled from her only chance left for housing after she ages out of foster care. She's left the room as immaculate as always. Her bed is made. Stuffed animals sit on her pillows. On her dresser I notice a pair of diamond earrings and walk closer to inspect them. I can't imagine why she's left something so valuable behind. I pick them up and realize they're cheap costume knockoffs.

Gladyce stares out the window. "This child is doing everything in her power to die on the streets."

Because I've been focused solely on the job, I've left little room for a social life. As a way to counter that, I go on a date with a man I meet on a social networking website. I haven't dated in years and am afraid I won't know how to read the subtle signs of flirtation or rejection. Cam is a boyish, articulate anthropology student, originally from the Virgin Islands. We decide to keep the evening casual and take a walk through Greenwich Village. We pass by curbside cafes and bong shops as we talk. I have a difficult time keeping eye contact as he tells me about his classes and growing up on the island. My voice feels shaky when telling him about the youth in my care and how I fell into doing this work.

We find ourselves walking to the Hudson River, standing at the lip of the water as boat lights gleam in the distance. A young trans girl struts past with a john twice her age and I realize I've unintentionally taken Cam to the piers where the residents go to stroll. Standing against the railing, looking out at the Hudson River softly lapping against the shore, I nod my head and smile as Cam talks, but I no longer hear his words. I'm consumed with thoughts of Bella, and where she might be.

It's getting late and the lulls in conversation are growing, so Cam and I make our way back toward the subway. We cross through the Village, where throngs of young queer kids populate the streets in front of bars, assembling in boisterous clusters. I'm surprised to find out that Cam is well versed in the difficulties gay kids of color face finding a space to exist in the city. We discuss the heated battle taking place in the neighborhood between mostly white homeowners and the mostly black and brown LGBTQ youth who gravitate nightly to the Christopher Street area. We agree that queer spaces need to become inclusive of all who identify as LGBTQ, not just the white middle-class males who are most visible. I feel myself finally loosening up. A genuine rapport seems to be growing. We begin to move past Ninth Avenue when I hear my name called out.

Raheem and Christina are waving from across the street.

"Ryan," Raheem says, bewildered, running up to us, "what you doing here?"

It's the first time any of the residents have seen me outside the context of the group home.

"Just going for a walk," I say.

Raheem and Christina both eye Cam. I make a clumsy introduction and it becomes clear I'm on a date. Raheem's face lights up.

"Ryan is the best caseworker ever," he says, a little too adamantly, as he gives Cam the once-over.

"Yeah!" Christina says, touching the collar of Cam's shirt. "The best."

Just then a hulking man walks up behind Christina, glaring at me. Christina puts her hand on the man's chest as if to calm him and explains that I'm her caseworker. The man's face softens.

"I'll be over by my bike," he says to Christina. "Let me know when you're ready." I ask who the man is and Christina gives me some half-baked answer about a family friend, avoids looking at me.

The streets are rowdy and caustic with drunks, and I'm reminded that Christina is only sixteen. "It's past curfew," I say. "You guys need to go home."

Both Raheem and Christina roll their eyes and laugh. They say goodbye and I tell them to be careful as they make their way across the street where the man is standing next to his Harley, watching us. As we walk away, I look back at them. They bend over the motorcycle with all the awe and joy of youth beaming from their faces. The man stands behind Christina, places a hand on her lower back, and steps closer to her. I stare until she meets my eye. She smiles as if to say, "I'm OK."

"That must be difficult," Cam says, "letting them go."

I tell Cam a fair amount of letting go is required, trusting that some of the information I've imparted has stuck with the residents. How we define risk is relative, and I can't always rein in their behavior. This work hardly ever produces immediate, desired results. The residents rarely meet the goals the program sets for them.

"Where's the reward when the outcome is almost always failure?" Cam asks.

I tell him about Jessica's response to the same question when I posed it to her in a moment of frustration. She told me about Japanese rock gardens, how when the monks finish their intricate design, they immediately begin to erase it, never giving themselves time to admire what they've just created. "The reward comes from the doing," she said, "not the result." The thing that is so profound to me about working at Keap Street is how my choices boil down to the essentials. Everything comes down to helping make someone's life a little less difficult. And in order to do so, I need to remain in the present. There's no hiding. Simply trying to connect with the residents, to be present in their lives, to continue to show up for them day after day, when no one else has—proving I won't disappear—forces me to remain present in my own life.

Cam and I stand at the West Fourth Street subway station, waiting for his train. He's staring down the tunnel with his hands buried in his pockets. I watch a rat try to smuggle a half-eaten burrito into a drainage pipe. When Cam's train finally arrives he steps toward the tracks, looks back, says it was nice meeting me. I smile halfheartedly.

"You have my number," he says, smiles, and disappears into the train. I know I won't have the confidence to call him and we won't see each other again.

Monday at the office I'm gathering my things for Junior's court hearing when my phone rings. I hesitate for a moment, knowing it'll be a new crisis that'll anchor me to the office for too long, but I can't stop myself from picking up. Gladyce is on the other end. Bella showed up at Keap Street, high from an epic crack binge. She's at Woodhull Hospital and will be released sometime tomorrow. I'm relieved Bella has surfaced. I thank Gladyce for the update, hang up the phone, and make my way out the door.

Later that day, I'm at Keap Street. Screams and laughter come from the kitchen on the floor above. Something heavy falls and the house shakes. More laughter, more screams. It's time for lunch and the residents are getting rowdy. On my way up from Gladyce's basement office I realize the staircase is banking more and more to the right. The plaster on the wall is cracked and peeling off in a thin strip. There could be internal water damage from when the sub-basement flooded last month. Gladyce probably called maintenance to check it out.

Before I get to the top of the stairs I can already smell the Jamaican beef patties in the oven mixing with the smell of Clorox the staff used to clean the floors. In the living room Christina is watching TV. She is wearing a black spaghetti-strap top, blue jeans, and pink Chinese slippers. She sits on one hip, her legs tucked up beside her.

"I think lunch is ready," I say.

On the couch across from Christina lies Caridad, face down, sprawled out, softly snoring. She's recently been sent to Keap Street from the 401 for a respite placement after too many AWOLs.

I tap her shoulder. "Time for lunch, Sunshine."

Caridad grunts, her face smeared with mascara. Her black fingernail polish is bitten down and chipped. She turns away from me and grumbles, "Go away." I notice she's still wearing the white pants we purchased for her job interview three days ago. They're gray now.

"You know I don't eat that ghetto shit," Christina says without taking her eyes off the screen. She then cranes her neck back and shines me a mischievous smile. "Honey, I'm strictly red carpet and don't you forget it." Her self-assuredness, her unwavering belief that she will transcend all that has held her back, makes me smile.

In the dining area, just outside the kitchen door, Maite and Junior sit at a cluster of small tables pushed together to make what is intended to be a larger dinner table for all twelve residents. At the center is a stack of plastic plates, plastic forks, napkins, and a deck of cards the youth use for playing spades after dinner. Junior is mixing a pitcher of powdered fruit drink. Outside the rain pelts the cement; a draft whispers in through the window.

"Give it to me." Maite reaches for the pitcher, but Junior moves it out of her grasp. She sucks her teeth. "You got to put more sugar in it, yo."

In the kitchen I see Crush with her arm pulled out of one shirtsleeve. Over her bare right shoulder blade is white gauze and medical tape covering the wound she suffered when a girl named PeeWee stabbed her for flirting with her girl. Crush uses her good arm to help Octavia scoop beef patties onto a serving tray. Typically, the staff adheres to a meal plan, but today Octavia and her co-workers had to contend with Crush returning with her stab wound, Junior's obstinate behavior, and a backed-up toilet overflowing onto the floor of the girl's bathroom. There was little time to prepare a decent lunch. The patties are piled on top of one another; iceberg lettuce with Italian dressing is mixed in a Tupperware bowl. Individual packs of Doritos are emptied out onto a plate. Octavia instructs Maite to help bring the food out to the table.

"This shit look mad nasty," Maite says, eyeing the browned skin of the beef patties. "I ain't eating this shit. Can't you make something people *wanna* eat? Why group home food always got to taste like ass?" I chisel through the patty with my plastic fork and knife. I don't want to eat it but am worried that I'll cause an uproar if I don't. I can hear Maite's voice in my head: "Oh, you too good for this shit but go ahead and serve it up to us?" Junior is standing in the corner by the kitchen door, stuffing salad in his face with his fingers. Most of it drops to his feet.

"Junior, use a plate, please," I say, "and clean up your mess."

He kicks the lettuce under the table. "Octavia'll get it," he says without looking up.

I'm about to respond when Maite looks up from the pile of Doritos she's chosen to eat in defiance. "You hear Bella's in the hospital, right?" she asks. Concern sweetens her face.

"Yeah, I just heard. Were you here when it happened?"

"Oh, man, she looked mad crazy." Maite sits up on her heels. "I was so scared, yo. I thought she was going to die." She looks down at her fingers, stained orange from the Doritos, and sticks two of them in her mouth. Christina enters the dining area and grabs a patty from the tray.

"Bitch deserves it," she says, and laughs. "You know you got a problem when your own crack pipe try and kill you." Before I know what's happening Maite has jumped across the table. I drop my plate and lunge forward, trying to intercept their collision. Luckily Junior is there to hold Maite back.

"I'm going to fucking kill you, bitch," Maite says. Her face is scarlet; her eyes, wild. She's fighting against Junior's restraint. "Who the fuck you think you are, anyway, bitch? Think you all high and mighty." Junior clutches Maite's shirt, holding tight. "Bitch, your moms shit you out of her pussy onto the sidewalk and left your black ass there. You ain't nobody." The sweetness has turned.

I stand in front of Christina and block Maite from her view. I can't remember the last time a whole day has passed without an altercation of some kind taking place, and I hope this one dissipates before we have to call the police. From the corner of my eye I see Octavia locking the kitchen door in case someone has the notion to grab a knife.

"Somebody forget her medication this morning? Where's the nurse? This crazy bitch needs her pills," Christina says, waving her beef patty overhead.

The phone rings. Could be Gladyce. Could be something she needs to tell me about Bella. I want to answer it but I know that I can't. Maite really wants to come to blows, this isn't just for show, and the other residential counselors are upstairs. I can't leave Octavia to deal with her alone. I move over to Maite to try and calm her down while the phone continues to ring out. Christina walks back to the living room talking about how this place is so ghetto.

"I'm sick of this shit," Junior says, shaking his head. "Everybody here always doing each other dirty." He bends down and picks the lettuce off the floor, scrapes it back on his paper plate, dumps it into the trash. He walks out of the kitchen. I can hear his voice trailing behind him.

"The fucked-up shit in this house could fill a motherfucking book," he says.

The Hell's Kitchen apartment Bella's thirty-year-old Jersey boyfriend promised her fell through. As a last resort we bring her to the 401. She's officially past her aging-out date, but Jessica has agreed to house her until another bed opens in the detox program. Keap Street is too fraught with temptation because Manhattan is just across the bridge and her dealers are all close by. We know there's no way she'll be able to stay sober there, even for a night. But we're afraid Bella will be tempted to flee in the night, so as a precautionary measure, I decide to sleep in the living room with her at the 401. So does Maite.

I haven't been back since I left almost a year ago. Nothing remains stagnant for long in places like this. Alexander and Montana are the only residents I recognize. We put blankets and pillows down on the floor and the couch. On TV a New York magician talks about his plan to submerge himself in a sphere of water for a week. Bella and Maite sit on the floor in their pajamas and quietly talk in Spanish. As I'm getting ready to turn out the light Bella turns to me.

"I want to be good, Ryan. I'ma really try."

Bella tells me she's going to save the money from a job she doesn't have, go to the Fashion Institute of Technology, and study design. She'll live in the dorms and have a roommate from the suburbs. "I'ma show everybody and become an interior decorator," she says. A few months ago I might have encouraged her fantasy, told her she's capable of anything. Now I only focus on ensuring she's not homeless.

"You can beat this, Bella," I say. "Work on beating your addiction and the rest will fall into place." My words sound hollow but I mean it.

When I wake the next morning I'm relieved to see Bella asleep on the floor beside me. She gets dressed and eats sugary cereal with the other residents. As I'm getting ready to hurry home and clean up quickly before running back to the office, she grabs my arm, smiles, and thanks me for staying with her. She gives me a hug, squeezes me tightly, her hair smelling like lemons. I walk to the door and wave back to her.

"Next time you see me, I'ma be clean and sober," she says, and gives a triumphant shake of her hair.

Two nights later, because no recreation is planned, I take a few of the residents from both the 401 and Keap Street out for dinner. They decide on the TGI Friday's in Times Square. I was hoping Bella and Christina could have joined us, but Bella slipped away from the 401 shortly after I left the house. Christina then disappeared from Keap Street. Neither one has been heard from since.

The restaurant is packed with tourists. The staff looks harried and tired. The host takes us to the second floor and slides three tables together. Benny and Montana flank me in the center, Reginald grabs a seat across from me, and Caridad sits at the end. Other customers stare at her shock of purple hair, black goth boots, and painted eyebrows. Our food comes and I watch Reginald eat his burger with a fork and knife "like white people do." Montana licks buffalo wings sauce off her fingers. We almost make it through the entire meal when we hear snickering coming from a group of young tourists a few tables away.

A teenager in a Toby Keith T-shirt becomes emboldened by the relative safety of his group, points to Caridad, and says, "What the fuck is that?" His group, huddled and clucking, explodes into laughter. I look to Caridad, tell her to ignore them. They're ignorant kids from some dingleberry town in the Midwest and not worth her time. "That should be locked up," the boy continues.

Caridad stands, and I place my head in my hands. "I know you ain't talking about me," she says, her voice thundering over the drone of customer chatter. Our waiter rushes over and asks her to keep it down. I lean in and tell him to address the real problem: that table of arrogant kids.

Caridad doesn't wait for an answer. She pushes past the waiter. "I'ma step into my hood skin for a second just so people don't forget," she says, then turns to address the boy. "Just 'cause you from out of town doesn't mean a nigga can't eat dirt, easy! Dick don't make a man. I'll crush you every day, asshole." The force and authority in her voice leaves me breathless. So many of the youth have learned to be fearless, standing up for themselves because no one else will. The room turns silent except for our table, which is whooping up a storm. The boy who was so loud a moment ago has buried his face behind a menu. Caridad sits down, puts her napkin in her lap, and looks over to me, smiling. "And I'm back."

I return with the residents to Keap Street to find Jessica and Gladyce in the living room.

"You're here late," I say.

Jessica's face is somber. "Can we have a word with you?" I look to Gladyce, who won't meet my eye.

"In private. Let's go to the office."

Panic grips me; my mind begins to race as we walk downstairs.

"Lock the door," Jessica says. "I don't want anyone barging in."

I do as I'm told and turn back to them. I try swallowing, but it feels like I have gravel in my throat.

"We have some bad news."

I sit in a chair as if on command, and white-knuckle the armrests.

"It's Bella," I hear Jessica say.

I exhale loudly.

"She didn't relapse, did she? She knows this is her last opportunity or she's on the street."

Jessica shakes her head.

"I wish it were that simple."

I'm told that Bella showed up tonight, shaken, high, while I was out to dinner with the other residents. She confessed she had been with Christina on the stroll two nights ago. A man approached them. Bella got a bad vibe from the guy and tried to distance herself. Bella told Christina she thought the guy was psycho, but Christina was blinded by the money and blew off Bella's warning. She went into a bodega with him to get cash from the

ATM. The last thing Bella saw was Christina getting into his car and heading up the West Side Highway.

I look at the grave expression on both of their faces. Christina has always been so self-assured, a powerful advocate for herself, seemingly wiser than the others in handling her sex-work transactions. When I couldn't get her placed into the school she wanted fast enough, she took it upon herself to register. Her fearlessness could come off as confidence, leaving staff to believe she was less in need than she actually was. Despite all the trouble she'd gotten into in the past—and her age, sixteen—I somehow allowed myself to believe she wouldn't fall victim to the allure of the street, the promises of fast money. She seemed too proud, too self-reliant for that. Overburdened, and overwhelmed with the needs of the other youth, I allowed myself to believe Christina's issues didn't require immediate attention because they often didn't present as a crisis. I took advantage of her self-determination; it provided some reprieve, some room to breathe. I wonder now if I stepped back too far from her.

Jessica sits still in the lamplight, her eyes heavy.

"I've called the police and the agency's private investigator. Things aren't looking good. He's been tracking Christina's phone and bank records. There's been no activity since she disappeared with the john two nights ago."

We spend the better part of the night making "MISSING" fliers with Christina's picture and statistics on them. Jessica, Gladyce, and Octavia go down to the piers on the West Side Highway where the residents typically stroll, and begin the search. I make up an excuse, tell them I can't go, grab a stack of fliers for later, and make my way for the subway. I have a foreboding ache in my gut and need to be alone for a while. The team starts at the bodega where Christina was last seen. Jessica texts me later as I sit alone beneath a rumbling overpass: there's a security camera at the bodega. They asked the clerk if it's functional and a wave of relief washes over me when she says it is. The clerk told them the police would have to come to retrieve the video.

When I arrive at the piers, it's late, and the city lights halo the treetops. I walk toward a porn shop where people are congregating and hand passersby fliers with Christina's information. Coming toward me is a man with salt-and-pepper hair. He's arm in arm with a boy no older than sixteen—Christina's age. As I stare at them, a deep sadness overcomes me. The boy notices me watching and gives me a twisted look as they pass, holding each other.

On May 30, 2005, Natalee Holloway disappeared during a high school graduation trip to Aruba a few months before Christina vanished. Her disappearance caused a media storm. With the help of hundreds of volunteers, Aruban investigators conducted an extensive search. The FBI and Dutch soldiers, along with high-tech Dutch aircraft, all participated in scrutinizing every inch of the island. In addition to the ground investigation, divers examined the ocean floor for evidence of Holloway's body. In the days following her disappearance, American media was ablaze with Holloway's image.

With Christina's disappearance, we can't even get the police to decide which precinct should begin the case. No one wants it. The precinct in Manhattan where she was last seen tells us we need to go to the precinct in the neighborhood where she resides. When we get to Brooklyn they tell us to go to Manhattan where the disappearance took place. She's well known at both precincts, considered a nuisance because of all the trouble she gets in, resulting in piles of paperwork. While getting the runaround I overhear one cop say to another, "One less tranny whore to deal with," then chuckle. The cop who is talking shit about her is red-faced and sweaty. I imagine asking the residents how many times he's taken advantage of girls like Christina, threatening to haul them off to jail if they refuse to go down on him. I imagine posting pictures of him around the neighborhood with his story. The information, I assume, would be appreciated.

We tell the police about the security camera at the bodega. They could review it, identify the man who was last seen with Christina. But there's an unmistakable disinterest on their part. They don't even pretend they're searching for her. One officer says, "She'll turn up. They normally do," without looking up from the papers he's thumbing through. *They normally do?* No, actually, they don't. Anyone who's watched a minute of local evening news knows that. It's unclear if the police ever look at the surveillance video. The missing persons report we file, papering the piers with her photograph, my appearance in front of a judge a few weeks later—these are the futile attempts at locating Christina. It seems as though the neglect she tried so hard to outrun her whole life is what spirited her away. Her coveted red carpet yanked out from beneath her.

I leave the police station disgusted. As I make my way to the subway in the muted gray afternoon, I want to find a place to hide from the city noise. I admonish myself for failing Christina, for not chasing her down, dragging her home at night kicking and screaming. I should have had one more conversation with her about her safety. I should have done more to protect her. I make my way underground, stand at the edge of the subway platform, surrounded by the stagnant heat and stink of the tunnel. A rush of wind comes into the station. Just before the train blasts in, I close my eyes and let the gushing air roar in my ears. I try to push, kick, thrust the thoughts of failing Christina out of my mind. When the subway doors release I open my eyes and search the sea of people, hoping to find her there, casually flipping her hair, staring back at me, telling me in her southern accent that she's ready, finally, to go home.

AFTERCARE

CHAPTER 9

GOING HOME

The funeral home is a converted storefront in Harlem. I'm sitting in the back row with Gena. When Octavia arrives, we both stand up and embrace her. It's 2012, six years since I've seen any co-workers from the LGBTQ program. It only took a few months after Christina's disappearance to decide I couldn't continue at Keap Street. We'd gathered the residents from both group homes for a meeting to talk about how they felt about Christina's disappearance. At first no one spoke up, all staring out with blank expressions. Finally, Benny broke the silence by saying, "Another person dead, so what? She fucking deserved it, stupid bitch." He started crying.

After two years of serving the youth walking in and out of the 401 and Keap Street, I quit to attend a graduate program. Leaving was difficult but also a relief. The residents' tireless adolescent antics and the accumulating tragedies of their lives became too much to handle. I felt ill-equipped to provide the level of care they deserved, unable to separate my worth from the ability to fulfill their needs. Successes did occur: Bella finally made it into detox, and Alexander graduated high school. But after Christina's disappearance I couldn't shake the feeling that I was only there to maintain a level of dysfunction until something else horrible happened. I've tried to stay in contact with a few of the youth, but with phone numbers constantly changing and canceled Facebook accounts, it's hard to keep up.

Caridad walks in the funeral hall pushing a stroller. Despite being visibly upset, she forces a smile and offers tepid hugs. She still has facial piercings like she did at Keap Street and the 401, but her hairstyle has mellowed with age. Instead of bright and fiery colors, she's settled on a washed-out, muted pink. Caridad introduces us to her young daughter, who's sucking on her fist, and her boyfriend, who stands behind her like a bodyguard. Jessica and Gladyce show up next. We embrace and struggle to smile. Raheem arrives just as the pastor begins the service. He scoots past a row of people, knocking a few knees on his way, eager to embrace each one of us.

Up in front, a small bouquet of flowers and a CD player sit on an end table. Next to that, a picture of Johnell, the young man with honey-colored eyes who aged out of care soon after I arrived at the 401, is on display. His family enters as a mournful gospel song plays through the speakers.

I reached out to Johnell on social media a few times over the years. I was compelled to check in on him after I'd come across a photography book in the East Village about gay male go-go dancers in New York. The book showed gritty backrooms, suggestions of illicit sex, parties, and drugs. Flipping through its pages, I saw dancers caught in risqué, frozen poses. The photographer suggested the subjects were "rough trade," men with criminal pasts, busted for prostitution, drugs, or assault. Others were "gay for pay," husbands with wives and kids, trying to scrape by. I was surprised when I came across a photograph of Johnell wearing nothing more than a G-string, his eyes spaced out, his body slick with sweat. Online, I'd asked him how things were going. He was blunt about his life after foster care. Finding stable housing was a consistent challenge. He'd been doing porn and dancing for money. I told him I'd seen him in the book, and expressed concern about his partying, drinking, and drug use, and how that might affect his ability to care for himself. In order to stay healthy it was crucial he adhere to a strict regimen of prescribed AIDS medication, which was difficult to maintain while thrust into the erratic life of a party boy. The Johnell I knew at the 401, although bright and quick-witted, was unable to manage his simple daily med intake without a prompt from staff. On his own, I feared he'd let his meds slide, or worse.

Although many of the youth I worked with, including Johnell, had lost parents to AIDS, there is a growing belief that contracting the disease is no longer a death sentence. The general sentiment now is that people can live with AIDS. This is true, but only with a considerable overhaul in daily routines. Even if a person is able to pay for the medication—a luxury many aging out of foster care can't afford—a litany of problems can arise. The drugs can have serious side effects, particularly in advanced stages of the disease; if patients miss doses, drug resistance can develop. In addition, providing antiretroviral treatment is resource-intensive, and individuals who fail to use antiretrovirals properly can develop multi-drug-resistant strains that can be passed onto others.

I asked Johnell if he was maintaining his meds and making his doctor appointments. He avoided my questions. I could tell by his posts and status updates that the youthful fire I'd encountered at the 401 was waning. Life had become more challenging and exhausting. Although he'd write messages like "Learning to love myself a little more each day," the pictures he posted showed just how difficult things had become since he left care. Gone were the wry smiles and bright eyes. He'd lost considerable weight, and the sharp angles of his face had grown more severe and extreme. There were vague posts about hospital visits. When I inquired about why he was hospitalized he neglected to elaborate. But he didn't need to. Everything left unsaid was made apparent when he suddenly vanished online. Friends posted messages asking if he was all right; they told stories of calling, leaving voicemails, and receiving no response. Some messages turned frantic, friends asking friends on his wall to provide some indication of Johnell's well-being. But no one was able to. In less than a decade after leaving foster care, still in the rush of his twenties, Johnell passed away.

The pastor stands at a small podium and wipes the sweat from his forehead. His face looks pained. He's talking about loving your brother, regardless of your prejudices. "We need to take care of our young people, not turn our backs on them," he says. He looks intently into the crowd of mourners. "You got to love each other, damnit."

He talks about Johnell's last days. They'd grown close over the past year, and Johnell had confided in the pastor. "He was so tired of fighting," the pastor said. "He wanted the constant struggle to stop. He wasn't afraid to die. He was ready to go home." A swell inside me grows. The pastor continues, "Everybody has within them the potential to find their goodness, their value, by searching for truth and overcoming trauma. If you're willing—it's not easy, but if you're willing, it can be done. Johnell was able to embrace that in his last moments."

I'm grateful he wasn't alone, that he had a confidant with whom he could talk. His life, like those of so many of the youth I worked with, was plagued by homophobia, both internalized and societal. Compound that with the racial and economic disparities they faced, and their associated liabilities—depression, anxiety, drug use, illness, violence, a ruined family life, systemic neglect—and the cycle feels endless. Sitting in a funeral home, seeing the chilling statistics I learned on the job play out in the tragic outcome of someone I worked with, is startling. I can't help wondering what we could have done differently.

A young transwoman is in front of me, rocking her baby, a child I hear her say she's acquired from an incarcerated sibling. Before the service I overheard her talk about Johnell, how they'd been friends at a group home previous to the 401. Other queer kids surround her. One is dressed in tight-fitting black leggings, another in sequins with glitter around his eyes. Standing near the back, young men with hard looks and sad eyes drape their arms around one another's shoulders. In the front row, near the picture of Johnell, sits his biological family. Behind them the rows are filled with his chosen family— the brothers and sisters he met at the piers, in the ball scene, in group homes and shelters, who all found one another out of necessity.

The pastor asks if anyone would like to say a few words. There's a moment of silence, then Raheem gets up, smoothes out his pants, and takes his place at the podium. He looks composed and self-assured. He clears his throat and addresses the group. He tells us how he'd met Johnell at the group home, how they grew tight fast, getting into trouble, making sure they kept things "turned up." He acknowledges that like Johnell, he too has tested positive for HIV. He too experienced the initial shame, then discrimination from his family and the community. Raheem talks about the importance of building support, so the secondary status of being black, poor, gay, and HIV-positive—and the pain that such a status proliferates—doesn't leave young men deprived and feeling forever devalued. He wishes Johnell had felt more empowered, had felt loved, and hopes that now he can finally rest.

After the service, everyone from the program is gathered in the foyer, catching up. I'm standing next to Raheem, who fills me in on the other former residents. Junior is living as a female now. Montana is in a homeless shelter. Benny stays to himself, but he's working, couch-hopping from friend to friend. Rumors are circulating that Reginald is doing porn, and maybe prostituting. Bella completed her stint in detox but soon lost her way again. Because she's older, tricks from the piers no longer want her, and she's been relegated to strolling in front of the projects in the South Bronx. She was last seen a year ago. When I ask about Christina, Raheem shrugs. No one heard from her again, and everyone assumes the worst. We settle into an awkward silence until he begins to talk about his new shoes, kicking one foot forward, admiring his purchase.

I glance up at Caridad holding her baby. She rocks back and forth, gently patting the child's back, coaxing a burp. Gladyce and Octavia crowd around her, leaning in, trying to glimpse the toddler's face. I overhear Caridad say she's living in a homeless shelter for mothers and their children. There's conversation about what progress she's made searching for assisted-living programs. They run through her options. In order for her to be eligible she needs to meet the requirements of the programs. There are restrictions on work, on school, on income. Watching them help Caridad strategize, it seems to me it should be so much simpler. Our duty was to shelter the youth in our care, but the brick and mortar of the 401 and Keap Street was only a piece of what the youth sought. Many found home in the relationships established with caring, consistent adults. Even though Caridad aged out years ago, Gladyce, Octavia, Jessica, Gena, and others remain a part of her life. They've stayed connected, and continue to show up for her. Knowing she still has that support seems to buoy Caridad, relieves a small part of the burden she carries.

What would it take to build on the small successes workers make with LGBTQ youth like Caridad? The system would need to look through a different lens, and acknowledge the interconnectedness of systemic racism, homophobia, transphobia, and poverty. LGBTQ foster kids need access to services that affirm their identities. Service providers have to be trained to see the youth from a trauma-informed perspective—a treatment framework that involves understanding, recognizing, and responding to the effects of all kinds of trauma—rather than doling out oppositional-defiant diagnoses to anyone who is argumentative and unruly. To help young people in care build their coping mechanisms, we not only have to treat symptoms, but also help them heal from the underlying cause of their behavior. Instead of shipping young people from placement to placement, we have to allow them to build attachments with caring adults. Maybe then they could have the opportunity for greater success, inching toward reducing harm in their lives instead of battling the dehumanizing ways the system treats them for being different. All youth deserve a safe place to live, yet queer-affirming foster homes can be challenging to find. This is not for a lack of trying. There are more than 2 million LGBTQ adults in the United States willing to foster or adopt, yet 60 percent of foster care agencies report never having placed a youth with LGBTQ couples, and 40 percent of agencies said they would not even accept applications from LGBTQ individuals or couples.[1]

What can be done to ensure LGBTQ youth transitioning out of foster care don't end up homeless? We need to deepen the conversation about homelessness and take action. Family rejection is a large part of the LGBTQ homeless youth narrative. A lot of ignorance and injustice has to be uncovered and put right. But we can't limit our discussion to an easily digestible sound bite. Simplifying the story to narrowly focus on rejection demonizes families and repairs little. Parents may need in-house guidance early on when they are struggling with a youth's identity. We can keep young LGBTQ people in their homes by providing preventive services and education to the parents. In addition to the family rejection narrative, we have to discuss institutional failures. Youth homelessness, in part, is the end product of the failure of other systems. We have to acknowledge how racial disparity—with its collateral consequences—interconnects with other predictors of homelessness. We have to build a social awareness so that folks who benefit from the system begin to realize that that very system is oppressive and threatening to others.

More beds in shelters are a temporary solution, a Band-Aid for a gushing wound. More must be done in the way of prevention so our young people won't need those beds to begin with. But in order for that to happen, we have to fully acknowledge how our systems often fail LGBTQ youth of color, and how institutionalized oppression makes it incredibly difficult for young people to find affordable, stable housing, get a job with a livable wage, and have an equal shot at the future they deserve.

I didn't know how much the program meant to the youth, or what a difference it made in their lives, until I recently came across an online post left by Gladyce. The note invited former youth and staff to a "Friends and Family Party" being held by the program. Initially, there were a few messages from former residents, inquiring about who would attend. Then Raheem and Fasheema began reminiscing about their time at Keap Street. "We ran that house," Raheem wrote. "Until Gladyce or Octavia caught us!" Suddenly the post was inundated with replies. Young people rallied to respond about their time at Keap Street, and the support the program provided them. Fasheema wrote, "I give it to Gladyce. She did her job and I hated that, but now I'm older with a child I understand it." Raheem replied, "She was old school! Gladyce, Octavia, and some of the old girls didn't play! They was on us. When Gladyce was working in the morning—I hated when I didn't want to go to school cause I knew when she was working 'it was on.' She don't play with disrespect, honey. She will turn up! Those days taught me a lot and very much prepared me for the 'Real World' after 21."

That was the first time I'd heard former residents comment on the program. I was deeply moved to know that a few of them felt they were bettered from their time at Keap Street. So was Gladyce. She responded, "You all are making me cry. It's so nice to see you all corresponding like this. I wish all of you could be there for the party."

Despite the shortcomings of the system, and the limitations it imposes on its workers, the people who actually show up to do the work, the people who invest in building vital relationships with youth every day, they are what make a difference. In our program I knew of only a few residents who aged out and went to college. Most had struggled to graduate high school or complete their GED. Research suggests that somewhere between 3 and 11 percent of former foster kids go on to graduate from college compared to 28 percent of the general population.[2] But personal fortitude and staff investment helped nudge some of the most accomplished young people who passed through our program to succeed despite the odds that piled up against them; they've attended graduate school, completed law degrees, and become impassioned advocates for marginalized populations.

I've been meeting up with one of those successes. Alexander, the young man who grew up in Pennsylvania and came to New York in search of a better life, started college in 2007. He's still writing, cobbling together enough time between classes and work to focus on his memoir. We've agreed to meet at a cafe in Brooklyn to look over his initial chapters. After years in the foster care system, where his story was dictated to him, he's learning to be the custodian of his own narrative. He has asked if I'd like to help him tell his story.

EPILOGUE

A decade has passed since I worked at Keap Street and the 401. Some improvements have been made since the events in this book took place, and systemic measures have been put in place to ensure the safety of LGBTQ youth in foster care. In 2008, thanks to the advocacy of the Sylvia Rivera Law Project, the Office of Children and Family Services (OCFS) in New York issued a new policy regarding LGBTQ youth. This new policy prohibits all OCFS staff, volunteers, and contract foster care providers from "engaging in any forms of discrimination against or harassment of youth on the basis of actual or perceived sexual orientation, gender identity, and gender expression."

OCFS also issued "Guidelines for Best Practices for LGBTQ Youth," which provide detailed explanations of what is considered appropriate treatment of LGBTQ youth in OCFS-operated residential and aftercare programs. These guidelines now support the rights of transgender youth—like Bella and Christina—involved in the juvenile justice system, allowing for gender-affirming name and pronoun use, gender-affirming clothing, and body searches by gender-appropriate staff. The new measures are in place, but it's difficult to gauge if they're being enforced.

Despite these small measures of success, the pipeline into homelessness continues. On a whole, there is much more work to be done. The U.S. government spends more than $5 billion annually on homeless assistance programs, yet roughly 5 percent is allocated to serve homeless youth and children.[1] There are steps the federal government can take to minimize the likelihood that LGBTQ youth leaving foster care will become homeless. Federal funding for essential services for LGBTQ youth remains frozen. Congress needs to reauthorize the Runaway and Homeless Youth Act, which would fund three major programs that provide critical services and support to our nation's homeless youth: Street Outreach; Basic Center (shelters); and Transitional Living Programs, demanding LGBTQ-specific protections barring discrimination. Congress must also establish principles to guard LGBTQ youth from bullying and harassment in schools; support preventive services that strengthen families with LGBTQ children and promote acceptance, education, and understanding; dismantle the school-to-prison pipeline; and initiate efforts for homeless youth research protocols that take into account and track LGBTQ youth demographic data including sexual orientation and gender identity. These federal efforts, in conjunction with state, city, and community efforts, could help ensure our youth have a chance at a brighter future.

I've since left New York and moved to Minneapolis. I currently work at Avenues for Homeless Youth, which provides two site-based shelter and transitional housing programs as well as the GLBT, Minneapolis, and Suburban Host Home Programs. The host home programs are an "outside the system" community and volunteer-based response to youth homelessness. Volunteers open their homes to young people looking for living stability, basic needs support, and healthy connections. Many youth seeking stable housing come out of foster care. Typically, youth have two overriding complaints about the foster care system: they had no say over where they were placed, and the people they lived with were paid to care for them. In our host home model, which is intentionally small and noninstitutional, these two features are flipped—the young person reads the applications of potential hosts and chooses whom to meet, and all hosts are volunteers. Host homes are thoroughly screened and trained, then provided ongoing support while they are hosting youth. But they are not "licensed," which provides flexibility to address changing needs as they arise. In addition to operating its programs for homeless youth, Avenues works to engage in the broader social justice movement, examine and challenge what causes and perpetuates youth homelessness, and communicate and advocate appropriately from its vantage point.

Precariously housed and homeless LGBTQ youth issues are as pervasive as ever. No one model alone will fix the problem. I've learned that what makes sense for me is to address youth homelessness on a community level. If I can show up, be consistent, and help build support systems within communities, perhaps my actions can make some small difference to someone.

ACKNOWLEDGMENTS

This book was made possible by the youth I worked with, who showed me the meaning of resilience, forgiveness, personal strength, determination, and courage.

I'm grateful to the journals where chapters of this book first appeared in slightly different forms: "Lady Fingers" in *Ploughshares*; "Tick Tick Boom" in *The Sun*.

I am greatly indebted to the following people for their support and guidance: Kathryn Harrison, Louise DeSalvo, Michael Taeckens, Ellery Washington, Adam Haslett, D.A. Powell, Richard McCann, Saïd Sayrafiezadeh, Nick Flynn, Meri Nana-Ama Danquah, Darin Strauss, Suzanne Snider, Eddie Sarfaty, Rachel London, Stephen Serwin, Joseph Espinal, Anna Marrian, Brooke Shaffner, Andrea Codrington Lippke, Manijeh Nasrabadi, Gwen Gunter, Rocki Simões, Jade Sanchez-Ventura, Debra Maeef, Rigoberto Gonzalez, Lee Ann Conlan, Gabriel Matthews, Dara Cole, Jennifer Gunnell, Sarah Mountz, Mark Sam Rosenthal, Mark Jaffe

ACKNOWLEDGMENTS

Cohen, Eli Ramirez, Amy Rhodes, Kathleen Delaney, Sam Citrin, Meghan Hatch, Linda Feldman, and Darcey Steinke. Thanks to the teachers of my youth, Carol MacVey, Jim and Cindy Lamson, and Julia Powell, for acknowledging and nurturing my voice. Thank you to Ron Starns and Anthony Capone for friendship, and keeping me employed throughout many years of writing. For the gift of artist residencies and financial support, endless thanks goes to: The MacDowell Colony, The Corporation of Yaddo, The Lambda Literary Foundation, and The New York Foundation for the Arts. The Hunter College Creative Writing MFA program was instrumental in the early stages of the writing process. Thank you to my agent, Ethan Bassoff, who believed in this book long before there was a book to believe in. Thank you to everyone at Nation Books, especially Dan LoPreto, Alessandra Bastagli, and Lindsay Fradkoff, for providing intelligent, compassionate attention to this project. Lastly, I want to thank my parents, Ron and Marty Berg. Because of their unconditional love and support, this book was made possible.

RESOURCE GUIDE

NATIONAL
National Runaway Safeline: 1800runaway.org
Homelessness Resource Center: homeless.samhsa.gov
The National Network for Youth: nn4youth.org
National Gay and Lesbian Task Force: thetaskforce.org
Forty to None Project: fortytonone.org

ALABAMA
Alabama GLBT Mentors: free2be.org

ALASKA
Identity: identityinc.org

ARIZONA
One•n•ten: onenten.org
Wingspan: wingspan.org

ARKANSAS
Lucie's Place: luciesplace.org
NWA Center for Equality: nwacenterforequality.org

CALIFORNIA
The Family Acceptance Project™: familyproject.sfsu.edu
The Pacific Center: pacificcenter.org
Los Angeles LGBTQ Center: lalgbtcenter.org
The LGBTQ Youth Space: defrankyouthspace.org
The Stonewall Alliance Center: stonewallchico.org
The San Diego LGBT Community Center: thecentersd.org

COLORADO
The Center: glbtcolorado.org
Urban Peak: urbanpeak.org

CONNECTICUT
Hartford Gay and Lesbian Health Collective: hglhc.org
True Colors: ourtruecolors.org

FLORIDA
ALSO Youth: alsoyouth.org
Compass: compassglcc.com
Orlando Youth Alliance: orlandoyouthalliance.org
Pridelines Youth Services: pridelines.org
SunServe: sunserve.org

GEORGIA
CHRIS Kids: chriskids.org
YouthPride: youthpride.org
Lost-n-Found Youth: lnfy.org

ILLINOIS
Project Fierce Chicago: projectfiercechicago.org
UCAN: ucanchicago.org
Affinity Community Services: affinity95.org

Howard Brown Health Center: howardbrown.org

INDIANA
Indiana Youth Group: indianayouthgroup.org

IOWA
United Action for Youth: unitedactionforyouth.org

KENTUCKY
Lexington Gay-Straight Alliance: lexgsa.org

LOUISIANA
Juvenile Justice Project: laccr.org/jjpl
LGBT Community Center of New Orleans: lgbtccnew
orleans.org

MAINE
Maine Youth Action Network: myan.org/about

MARYLAND
Rainbow Youth Alliance: rainbowyouthalliancemd.org
GLBT Community Center: glccb.org

MASSACHUSETTS
Boston Alliance of GLBT Youth: bagly.org
Boston GLASS Community Center: jri.org
The Home for Little Wanderers: thehome.org

MICHIGAN
The Neutral Zone: neutral-zone.org
Ruth Ellis Center: ruthelliscenter.org
TransYouth Family Allies: imatyfa.org

MINNESOTA

GLBT Host Home Program: avenuesforyouth.org/programs
-glbthosthome.html
Reclaim!: reclaim-lgbtyouth.org
The Bridge for Youth: bridgeforyouth.org
YouthLink: youthlinkmn.org
Face to Face: face2face.org
The Family Partnership: thefamilypartnership.org
Shades of Yellow: shadesofyellow.org

MISSOURI

Growing American Youth: growingamericanyouth.org
Passages: kcpassages.org
LIKEME Lighthouse: likemelighthouse.org

MONTANA

The Western Montana Community Center: gaymontana.org

NEVADA

The Center: thecenterlv.org

NEW JERSEY

Crossroads Programs: crossroadsprograms.org
The Pride Center of New Jersey: pridecenter.org
Newark LGBTQ Community Center: newarklgbtqcenter
.org/about-us

NEW MEXICO

Transgender Resource Center of New Mexico: tgrcnm.org

NEW YORK
Trinity Place Shelter: trinityplaceshelter.org
Ali Forney Center: aliforneycenter.org
New Alternatives: newalternativesnyc.org
Sylvia Rivera Law Project: srlp.org
Safe Horizon: safehorizon.org
Audre Lorde Project: alp.org/about
HEAT: heatprogram.org/lgbt.html
Gay Alliance: gayalliance.org
Pride Center of the Capital Region: capitalpridecenter.org
SCO Family of Services: sco.org/programs
/independent-youth
Green Chimneys: greenchimneys.org
The Door: door.org/programs-services/lgbtq
Hetrick-Martin Institute: hmi.org
Staten Island LGBT Community Center: pridecentersi.org
FIERCE: fiercenyc.org

NORTH CAROLINA
Haven House Services: havenhousenc.org
LGBT Center of Raleigh: lgbtcenterofraleigh.org
Inside Out: insideout180.org/about
Time Out Youth: timeoutyouth.org

OHIO
LGBT Community Center of Greater Cleveland:
lgbtcleveland.org
Rainbow Area Youth: raytoledo.org
Kaleidoscope Youth Center: kycohio.org

OKLAHOMA
OKC Youth United: okcyu.org
Openarms Youth Project: openarmsproject.org
Youth Services of Tulsa: yst.org/yst/History_of_YST.asp

OREGON
Sexual & Gender Minority Youth Resource Center:
    smyrc.org
Outside In: outsidein.org

PENNSYLVANIA
The Attic Youth Center: atticyouthcenter.org

RHODE ISLAND
Youth Pride, Inc.: youthprideri.org

SOUTH CAROLINA
We Are Family: waf.org

SOUTH DAKOTA
Black Hills Center for Equality: bhcfe.org
The Center for Equality: thecenterforequality.org

TENNESSEE
OutCentral: outcentral.org
Memphis Gay and Lesbian Community Center: mglcc.org

TEXAS
Out Youth: outyouth.org
Youth First Resource Center: myresourcecenter.org/
    what-we-do/community/youth-first

UTAH
Utah Pride: utahpridecenter.org

VERMONT
Spectrum: spectrumvt.org
Outright Vermont: outrightvt.org

VIRGINIA
ROSMY: rosmy.org
Diversity Richmond: diversityrichmond.org

WASHINGTON
Labateyah Youth Home: unitedindians.org/programs/
    youth-home/united-indians-homeless-youth-home/
YouthCare: youthcare.org
Lambert House: lamberthouse.org
Oasis Youth Center: oasisyouthcenter.org

WASHINGTON, D.C.
Advocates for Youth: advocatesforyouth.org
SMYAL: smyal.org
TransGender Education Association, Inc.: tgea.net/about

WISCONSIN
LGBT Center of SE Wisconsin: lgbtsewisc.org
MKE LGBT Community Center: mkelgbt.org

NOTES

NOTES TO PREFACE

1. James Baldwin, *Giovanni's Room* (New York: Dell Publishing, 1956), 121.

2. Ariel Leve, "Toni Morrison on Love, Loss and Modernity," *The Telegraph*, July 17, 2012.

3. The AFCARS Report, No. 19 (Washington, D.C.: U.S. Department of Health and Human Services, Administration for Children and Families, Administration on Children, Youth and Families, Children's Bureau), estimates as of July 2012.

4. Dave Reynolds, "Foster Kids Experience Far More Trouble as Adults, Study Shows," *The New Standard*, April 8, 2005.

5. Diane Mastin, Sania Metzger, and Jane Golden, "Foster Care and Disconnected Youth: A Way Forward in New York," Community Service Society/The Children's Aid Society, April 2013, at www.childrensaidsociety.org/files/upload-docs/report_final_April_2.pdf.

6. Mimi Laver and Andrea Khoury, "Opening Doors for LGBTQ Youth in Foster Care: A Guide for Lawyers and Judges," American Bar Association, 2008, at www.americanbar.org/content/dam/aba/administrative/child_law/2008_Openingdoors_Text.authcheckdam.pdf.

7. Robert B. Hill, "Institutional Racism in Child Welfare," in *Child Welfare Revisited: An Africentric Perspective*, eds. Joyce Everett, Sandra P. Chipungu, and Bogart R. Leashore (New Brunswick, NJ: Rutgers University Press, 2004).

8. Cris Beam, *To the End of June: The Intimate Life of American Foster Care* (New York: Houghton Mifflin Harcourt, 2013), 61–62.

9. Jaime M. Grant et al., "Injustice at Every Turn: A Report of the National Transgender Discrimination Survey," National Center for Transgender Equality and National Gay and Lesbian Task Force, 2011, at www.endtransdiscrimination.org/PDFs/NTDS_Report.pdf.

10. Audre Lorde, *Sister Outsider: Essays and Speeches* (Berkeley, CA: Crossing Press, 2007), 138.

11. Alex Morris, "The Forsaken: A Rising Number of Homeless Gay Teens Are Being Cast Out by Religious Families," *Rolling Stone*, September 3, 2014.

12. Andrew Cray, Katie Miller, and Laura E. Durso, "Seeking Shelter: The Experiences and Unmet Needs of LGBT Homeless Youth," Center for American Progress, September 26, 2013.

NOTES TO CHAPTER 5

1. Andrew Cray, Katie Miller, and Laura E. Durso, "Seeking Shelter: The Experiences and Unmet Needs of LGBT Homeless Youth," Center for American Progress, September 26, 2013.

2. Fred H. Wulczyn et al., "Foster Care Dynamics, 2000–2005: A Report from the Multistate Foster Care Data Archive," Chapin Hall Center for Children at the University of Chicago, December 2007.

NOTES TO CHAPTER 6

1. Jaime M. Grant et al., "Injustice at Every Turn: A Report of the National Transgender Discrimination Survey," National Center for Transgender Equality and National Gay and Lesbian Task Force, 2011, at www.endtransdiscrimination.org/PDFs/NTDS_Report.pdf.

2. Stephen T. Russell and Kara Joyner, "Adolescent Sexual Orientation and Suicide Risk: Evidence From a National Study," *American Journal of Public Health,* August 2001.

NOTES TO CHAPTER 9

1. Gary J. Gates, et al., "Adoption and Foster Care by Gay and Lesbian Parents in the United States," the Urban Institute and the Charles R. Williams Institute on Sexual Orientation Law and Public

Policy, March 2007, at http://www.urban.org/uploadedpdf/411437
_adoption_foster_care.pdf.

2. Cris Beam, *To the End of June: The Intimate Life of American Foster Care* (New York: Houghton Mifflin Harcourt, 2013), 98.

NOTES TO EPILOGUE

1. Alex Morris, "The Forsaken: A Rising Number of Homeless Gay Teens are Being Cast Out by Religious Families," *Rolling Stone*, September 3, 2014.

INDEX

INDEX

INDEX

Ryan Berg is a Lambda Literary Foundation Emerging Writers Fellow and received the New York Foundation of the Arts Fellowship in Nonfiction Literature. His work has appeared in *Ploughshares, Local Knowledge,* and the *Sun*. Ryan has been awarded artist residencies from the MacDowell Colony and Yaddo. He lives in Minneapolis.

The Nation Institute

Founded in 2000, **Nation Books** has become a leading voice in American independent publishing. The inspiration for the imprint came from the *Nation* magazine, the oldest independent and continuously published weekly magazine of politics and culture in the United States.

The imprint's mission is to produce authoritative books that break new ground and shed light on current social and political issues. We publish established authors who are leaders in their area of expertise, and endeavor to cultivate a new generation of emerging and talented writers. With each of our books we aim to positively affect cultural and political discourse.

Nation Books is a project of The Nation Institute, a nonprofit media center dedicated to strengthening the independent press and advancing social justice and civil rights. The Nation Institute is home to a dynamic range of programs: the award-winning Investigative Fund, which supports groundbreaking investigative journalism; the widely read and syndicated website TomDispatch; the Victor S. Navasky Internship Program in conjunction with the *Nation* magazine; and Journalism Fellowships that support up to 25 high-profile reporters every year.

For more information on Nation Books, The Nation Institute, and the *Nation* magazine, please visit:

www.nationbooks.org

www.nationinstitute.org

www.thenation.com

www.facebook.com/nationbooks.ny

Twitter: @nationbooks